Is God Enough?

One woman's journey through gain and loss

Becky Dietrich

DEDICATION

to my husband Mike,

my best friend, my rock, my cohort;

and to Jedd and Tyler,

my sons with warrior hearts

Contents

PROLOGUE

The skies are gray, the rain is falling. It is the dog days of summer in Seattle. The rented U-haul truck is loaded with everything we own. I look back at the little house we purchased so eagerly three and a half years ago; the little house with the "Welcome" plaque on the front door; the little house with the big granite island where our grandchildren had so often perched on stools awaiting family dinner; the little house where we so loved to welcome and serve people; the little house that we poured our life savings into and that was going to constitute our retirement nest egg; the little house that is no longer ours, that is being foreclosed on, that we are being forced to move out of. The Court has gone over our assets and liabilities with a fine tooth comb and has made it official. We are bankrupt. My husband Mike and I are both 60 years old. He is unemployed, and years of stress and strain on his back have left him essentially disabled. This is not a situation I ever pictured we would be in as we approached retirement.

I am embarrassed. Chagrined. Perplexed. Stupefied. Angry. Angry is not strong enough. LIVID is more like it. Livid at God.

It's like we have been racing downstream in a frigidly cold river swollen with floodwaters, riddled with rapids, and clogged with logs and rocks and snags. After a mighty struggle to stay afloat, our canoe has overturned, and we are gasping, spitting, flailing, screaming for help, and no one is answering. Especially and particularly God is not answering.

How, how did this happen?! How did I get from such a promising start to flat broke, old, and homeless...

1 BEGINNINGS

I was born supremely confident. Others have named it differently, "insufferably arrogant" probably topping the list. I was the third of four children born to loving committed parents in a faith based home. I essentially came out of the womb singing great hymns of the faith and reciting the Catechism - Westminster, of course.

We lived on a little bit of acreage on Vashon Island, a ferry ride away from Seattle, with my paternal grandparents. My grandmother would have made a magnificent 21st century woman. She was intelligent, strong minded, comfortable in her own skin. She loved interior design, and the arts, and hospitality. She had been briefly married in the first decade of 1900, but, unheard of in those days, got a divorce. My family never talked about it, so I don't know if she was escaping an abusive relationship, or if there was a less horrid reason. Then she met my grandfather, who worshipped the ground she walked on, and the air she breathed. They were in vaudeville together, then my father was born and they settled down to raising a family. In one of my favorite pictures of her she is wearing a preposterously broad brimmed Victorian hat, with feathers and plumes, and a print dress, looking as if she were queen of all she surveyed. Then there is the picture at my father's christening. Grandma Eloise is sitting, with my father in her lap. He is wearing a handmade white lace and ruffled christening dress that cascades almost to the floor. My grandfather is standing to the side, with his arm on the back of the chair, leaning over them. He has eyes only for them. The picture over my nightstand is of her in later years. The hat is smaller, the demeanor the same, but you can see the strain of chronic illness in her eyes. She had a very rare kidney disease. Only five people in the world ever had it, and three of them were in her family. She had to go to California when my father was a little boy for treatment, and was gone almost a year. When my father died, we found the letters between my grandparents from that time. Their passionate, earthy, vibrating love for each other, and their equally passionate faith in Jesus sang off the pages. The letters were so intensely personal that I put them away. They were not meant for anyone but themselves to read.

When I was seventeen days old, my Grandmother died.

And there I was, a living breathing, lusty, fat, crowing, healthy clone of her. Everyone, except me, knew that I would be my father's favorite.

When I was a few years old I was tested for the family disease and given a clean bill of health. As it has not reappeared in any generation since, I give totally unscientific credit to the undiluted gene pool of the brown skinned gentleman in full Indian headdress in one of the family pictures from the late 1800's. I discovered the picture when I was a teenager, tucked away in a chest of treasured family photos that belonged to my grandfather. When I showed it to my parents they did not want to talk about it, and although I pressed them for details, none were forthcoming. My curiosity led to the disappearance of the picture. But every generation one or two of us "throwbacks" pop up, like my grandmother and me, slightly dark skinned, with the ability to tan like a native.

My dad got quite ill after my grandmother's death, and ended up in the hospital. When my mom came to visit him, she would deposit me, still mercifully immobile, on his tummy, and go run errands. Apparently my presence in the men's surgical ward caused a few double takes from passers by. When Dad was well enough to come home, he would help Mom out by plopping me, cradle and all, in front of the old hi-fi. He would turn on his favorite music full volume. I think even then I reveled in Tchaikovsky, and Beethoven, and Rachmaninoff, and Gilbert and Sullivan. And the bond between me and my dad deepened.

My personality type makes for a rather exuberant baby, and a monstrous toddler. In pictures with my grandfather at a few months old,

I wouldn't stop trying to pull out his hair. After doing a number in my diapers, if my mom did not respond in a time-frame to my liking, I simply removed my diaper, and spread the contents on the nursery wall. When they tried to limit my activities to the play pen, I methodically loosened and removed enough slats to escape. My parents and siblings soon developed a mantra: "First there was the light bulb, then the automobile, then the radio, and now Becky." My mom would say that she had three normal children, and Becky. My dad would say "She's frequently wrong, but never in doubt."

I was actually ok with their teasing. I felt supremely loved. Mom would look at me with a wistful smile, and say "You are just like your grandmother."

I was in my middle 50's before I realized that my brother, who was more than eight years my senior, viewed my dad very differently than me. He was the first born, the namesake, and the only son. He was scary smart. I mean top of his law school smart. Given football or chess he would choose chess. Give him fishing, he would choose debate team. He was the classic nerd. The desk in his little room in our home - by now we had left the Island for more convenient living in Seattle - contained a file box detailing the exact location of everything of any importance to him. He was not dark and handsome like the ethnically mixed side of the family - my dad's side - but pale and blond like my 100% Norwegian mom. My older sister was born fifteen months after him, and she adored him. He was perfect to her. But he never felt good enough for my dad, or hairy enough, or muddy enough. He never felt like our dad approved of him. And then I came along, in some ways my father's boy. I was definitely my father's favorite, or so my brother perceived. Plus, he had lost a beloved grandmother and gained a lousy sister. It didn't help that a couple of years later our last sibling arrived, a little girl who shared my older sister's view of my brother. It was clearly my job to torment him, and I was very good at it.

We are so different, my brother and I. Where he would say, "Why doesn't my dad love me?", I would say "Everybody loves me, what's not to love!" Where I name my father as my hero, he is more likely to name him a stranger. If my brother would say "sit", I would stand...and stick my tongue out. There was nothing he said that I would not challenge. We have equally strong personalities, mine bold and exuberant, his passive but steely determined. It is no wonder our swords crossed. He left for college when I was about nine, but my mom would threaten me for weeks before he came home on breaks... "Be NICE to your brother!"

Years and years went by in which he barely tolerated me. It took the death of my dad for us to start talking, and now we have been able to come to a better understanding of, and a real love for each other. My brother had a long and illustrious career as a prosecutor. It was easy for my dad to talk to me about how proud he was of him. But as with many men of his generation, it wasn't easy for him to tell my brother what he told me. But it is easy for me. And I hope that, having shared these things with my brother, he will come to know and maybe even embrace the dad I knew. For now I am delighted that he embraces me.

2 CRACKS

I must have been about seven when I claimed my family's faith as my own. I clearly remember that night in church when the visiting preacher asked anyone who wanted to place their faith in Jesus to stand up and walk down the aisle to the front of the church. There was no way I was going to avail myself of such public scrutiny, but I sat in my seat, and prayed the prayer that invited Jesus to "come into my heart" and to walk with me the rest of my days. I don't remember feeling any different, only a little bit happier, if that were possible.

At about the same time, we got a television. This was the mid 1950's, and TV was a big deal. Our family rules regarding the television were quite simple. The TV was turned on once a week, for one show only. "Father Knows Best". My dad loved that show, and that was the one we were allowed to watch. No cartoons, no variety shows, just "Father Knows Best". The rest of our family time was spent reading books and listening to music. And my little sister and I would spend hours plopped in front of the furniture sized radio listening to the stories of the Lone Ranger, and his pal Tonto. That was my favorite radio show, and as soon as the heart pounding strains of the William Tell Overture poured out of the radio, I was transported to the dust and sun and sweat and honor of the Old West.

It was a wonderful childhood, and my relationship with my dad was the foundation of it. After my older siblings left for college, Dad worked very hard on spending time with my little sister and me. On Sunday afternoons after dinner he would take us on a long walk, down the dirt road behind our house, through what we affectionately called the gully, to the beach, where we would skip rocks and talk about life, and our faith, and what we believed. It is hard to overstate what an impact that kind of fathering had on me. My dad loved me unconditionally, and without reserve, and when you add that quality of love to the confident and assured personality I was born with, you end up with a pretty formidable person. I felt not only absolutely loved, but worth it.

In our home, we were - encouraged is too soft a word, commanded is too strong - to evidence our love for Jesus by several external behaviors. These included the major "no no's" of the Christian church; no smoking, no swearing, no dancing, no movies, no drinking, and no going out with boys that did.   I accepted that we acted a certain way to show that we believed in Jesus, but was still too young to grasp the elephant in the living room.   Didn't Jesus Himself say that obeying rules and regulations like the Pharisees of his day *did not* win his approval? Didn't Jesus go out of his way to confront and countermand every attempt the religious rulers made to force Him into their mold of outwardly respectable behavior? Didn't Jesus say that love defines the one who believes and walks with Him, not a list of taboos? Then something happened that shone the first light of my young life on the crack in my parents credibility.

Charlton Heston thundered onto the big screen as "Ben Hur".

Suddenly, movies were no longer a "no-no". I was totally delighted with this deletion from the black list, but wondered if it wasn't lovely and convenient that when all of a sudden there was a movie my parents wanted to see, the behavior necessary to be in relationship with Jesus changed as well. You might say, well maybe Ben Hur was ok because it told the story of Jesus. Nice try, but "The Sound of Music" and "How the West Was Won" became ok too. Next my dad started having digestion issues, and there went the "no drinking" taboo. Turns out that a little wine really is good for the stomach. The fact that the Apostle Paul had suggested exactly that remedy in his letter to Timothy in the Bible apparently had not provided a good enough excuse for imbibing before Dad's ailment took hold. Actually, was flummoxed. I had no idea why Paul's advice had not been good enough all along. But it was definitely still not good enough for my grandfather, because Dad carefully hid the wine in the very back of the refrigerator whenever Grandpa came to stay with us.

However the removal of the movie taboo led to one of my most memorable talks with my father. "Gone With the Wind" had been brought back into theaters, and was playing at the movie house in our neighborhood. I had heard of the wonderful, painful love story between Rhett and Scarlet, and I was dying to see the movie. So my dad and I had a "Gone With the Wind" date. I sat in my theater seat crying and laughing, and gasping, totally enthralled, completely buying into the concept that this was what true love was all about. As we walked home after, I started raving to my father about what a fabulous love story it was. He let me talk for a bit, then he stopped walking, looked me in the eye, and said "Whatever that was, it had nothing to do with love." My mouth must have dropped. He went on. "Scarlet and Rhett's relationship had to do with lust, and sex, and selfishness, and gratification for a moment, but it had nothing to do with true love. Love, real lasting love, is demonstrated when you care more for the needs of another person than for your own needs. Real love is demonstrated when you continue to act lovingly towards your partner, even if you are *not* feeling like you love him at the moment." Dad went on to quote from I Corinthians 13 in the Bible. "Love is patient, love is kind. Love does not envy, does not boast, is not jealous or proud. Love does not demand its own way. Love never gives up, never loses faith, is always hopeful, endures through every circumstance." My dad had nailed the problem with the kind of "love" portrayed by Hollywood, and had totally and irrevocably ruined "Gone With The Wind" for me. But he had given me something invaluable that would stick with me the rest of my life - a vision for what a truly loving relationship would look like.

3 TRUE TRUTH

I made a rather deplorable "child of the sixties." I didn't tune in, turn on, or drop out. I didn't do drugs. I felt no need to burn my bra. I didn't rebel against my parents and join a commune. But I did start to question what I had been taught since infancy. I was no longer willing to believe something just because my parents said it. I wanted to know if this whole ball of wax I had been fed my whole life was actually true. The struggle of my life would become "Is God enough?", but first I had to know "Is God?"

Ok, obviously this did not all occur to me in one great series of blinding flashes. I didn't find out Dad was taking us to Ben Hur and immediately start to doubt the veracity of my faith. But as I matured, year after year, in a quiet moment the questions would start to come.

One of the things I appreciate most about the God of the Bible is that unlike the gods of other religions, He likes to be questioned. In fact, He assures us that if we seek Him out, if we want to know who He is, if He is, and how we can know He is, He will find us and answer us. Jeremiah chapter 29 verses 13-14 affirm this. "You will seek me and find me. When you seek me with all your heart, I will be found by you..." And I wanted to know.

It was my senior year when God met me in the lecture auditorium of my very small private high school. On to the stage stepped an intense character of a man. He was clad in knickerbockers, with somewhat longish hair, and heavy horn rimmed glasses. Whenever he got excited, he'd rip off his glasses and the hair on the sides of his head would shoot out like he'd put his finger in a socket, and when the glasses returned to their place, his hair duly followed suit. Glasses off, bad hair day; glasses on, good hair day. The more passionate he became about his subject, the higher his voice got. He was mesmerizing, enlightening, challenging, liberating, and electrifying. His name was Francis Schaeffer, and he and his wife spent their lives in a chalet in

Switzerland inviting into their living room people from all over the world and from myriad different circumstances. They would show up on their doorstep wanting answers to the basic questions of life. Hippies, intellectuals, European nobility, opera stars, drug addicts, American dropouts, rich or poor. Anyone seeking answers was welcome. Now God had brought him from Switzerland to the doorstep of my high school.

In his lectures he confronted the American Church with its hypocrisy. "Love?!?!" he would shout. It was the sixties, after all. "Love!?! You don't know anything about love until you have drunks vomiting on your carpet, and burning your draperies with their cigarettes. Unless you open your home to people in need, SHUT UP about love!" And about racism, again, it was the 60's; "Shut up about the blacks! Unless you have them over for dinner, unless your children are playing together, unless you are hand in hand, shut up about the blacks!" He was a great theologian and philosopher, and he communicated truth in a powerful way.

His word from God to me related to the question that I was grappling with. Was what my parents believed true? And I mean *really* true, not just "true for them" or "true for me". Not the "whatever works for you" nonsense. I'm talking about truth in the classic, non-relative sense; truth in which "if A is true, the opposite of A is not true." Call it TRUE truth if you want. Or absolute truth. The kind of truth that is true for everyone, everywhere, all the time. The kind of truth the Christian faith espouses and lays claim to. I wanted to know if this Christian thing was really what it claimed to be - not just a religion, but the truth. After all, Jesus said "I am the way, and the truth, and the life, and no one comes to the Father but through me."

I was asking the kind of questions everyone of us must ask ourselves - and find the answer to - if we dare to lift the edges of the bed covers in the morning. This is where Schaeffer captured my attention. In his lectures that week at my high school he helped me by defining my questions, and positing the possible answers.

My first question had to do with existence and personality. Not just why do I exist, but why do I exist as a personal being?

Over the last few centuries, as our world progressively abandoned the Bible and the God of the Bible, various philosophies and philosophers have tried to address this question. They all understood the reality that without a personal God, there is no explanation for human personality. When I say personal, person-ness, or personality, I mean that we humans think. We are creative. We love and hate. We have moral inclinations. We make free choices, and we are held morally responsible for those choices. Our experience shows us that man is personal, in contrast to that which is impersonal, or animal, or machine. So when philosophers deny the existence of God, they have to postulate a personal man from an impersonal beginning. They have to explain how, since there is no God, everything that exists, including man, is the result of the impersonal, plus time, plus chance. This opens quite a can of worms.

First, no one has ever been able to demonstrate with any feasibility how an impersonal beginning can result in personality. To quote Schaeffer; "Because these men will not accept the only explanation that can fit the facts of their own experience, they become metaphysical magicians. No one has presented an idea, let alone demonstrated it to be feasible, to explain how the impersonal beginning, plus time, plus chance, can give personality. We are distracted by a flourish of endless words, and lo, personality has appeared out of the hat." Whether it is rationalism, or pantheism, or mysticism, none give a reasonable answer to person-ness. Only Biblical Christianity has an adequate and reasonable, cause and effect explanation for the source of human personality. The Biblical answer is that everything which exists was created by the infinite, personal, triune God. In historic Christianity a personal God - one who thinks, acts, creates, loves, chooses, asserts moral absolutes - created man in his own image. In the observable universe of cause and effect that's really there, the only reasonable explanation for a personal man is that he was created by a personal God.

To see the logic of this laid out for me was so exciting! I was beginning to see that my faith was not some archaic relic from an irrelevant past, but the actual timeless truth that made the pieces of life all fit together. I lived 20 miles from my high school, but after that first lecture, I was so excited that I went home every afternoon after school, and then drove back for Schaeffer's evening lectures.

He went on to explain that some anti-God thinkers see that personality requires a personal God so they try to assert that man is *not* personal. He is only animal or machine. The problem with this is that even the most stolid of thinkers can see this simply does not fit the facts of our own experience. If you look at the arts and the sciences from man's earliest attempts, you are deluged by the seminal creativity and personality exhibited. A cursory look at humans and how we relate shows clearly that love and hate are real. All of us experience personality in multiple, tangible, existential ways. We cannot live as if we were non-personal - as if we were animal or machine. We cannot help but stop and drink in a stunning sunset. We cannot help falling in love. We cannot help exclaiming over a beautiful baby, or a perfect pair of red shoes, or an unbelievable baseball catch. I remember when Ichiro Suzuki first came to the Seattle Mariners from Japan. He was an unknown to most of us fans, and we were eager to see what kind of stuff he had. It was early in his first season. My husband Mike and I were watching on TV. (I am the sports fan, Mikey tolerates me.) A ball was hit past Ichiro into the nether reaches of right field. The runner on first took off like a shot, rounded second, and was digging for third. Ichiro, having caught up with the ball, turned and let loose a throw, an unbelievably accurate, lightening fast throw that reached all the way from deep right field to third base, in time for the third baseman to tag the runner out. All 50,000 people in the stadium rose to their feet as one, in a throaty, ecstatic roar of approval. It has gone down in the annals of baseball lore simply as "the throw". This is human personality. Tomatoes don't revel in things like that, neither do tractors, or even house cats. We humans simply ooze with personality, and that cannot be explained by god-less philosophies. Only the Biblical answer has a sufficient explanation for this, and to believe otherwise is a giant leap of faith with no foundation in reason or observable fact.

An impersonal beginning in which there is no personal God has enormous implications, because man is left without any meaning. If man is thrown up out of the primordial ooze by chance and chance alone, then there is no meaning to his personality or his existence. Hope of purpose and significance, love, moral inclinations, rationality, beauty, and communication, are all unfounded and thus meaningless, if we exist by chance. Everything is finally chaotic, irrational, and absurd. And for most people, at least those who are thoughtful and sensitive, it doesn't take long after a little high school Darwinism, and college existentialism, to figure out the logical conclusion of an impersonal universe, and end up squarely in despair.

Despair! I totally got this. Even as a young teenager, I could see that if this stuff about God wasn't true, life was a pretty dismal proposition. Schaeffer named it "falling below the line of despair." In other words, there is nothing optimistic, happy, bright, hopeful or fulfilling in an impersonal universe. If you really face it square on, you only end up with darkness and death. If man is an animal or a machine, YOU are not really there. Personality is an illusion. Love is a joke. Goodness, mercy, justice, kindness - nothing but a silly vapor of self-deception. Man's efforts at civilization and civility are a study in futility. This is the logical conclusion if we begin with the impersonal plus time plus chance.

Do you really question, under the circumstances, why so many people do everything they can to shut their eyes against the awful blackness around them? Earn as much money as you can, eat, drink, be merry, die. The most you can hope for is a life of quiet desperation, followed by annihilation. Why shouldn't you grab for drugs, drink, sex, money, fitness, shopping, pornography, technology...any narcissistic self-indulgence to bring a modicum of comfort for a moment, if indeed there is no Personal beginning, and therefore no meaning or purpose in life? But this brought up the next big issue. What about morality, or moral absolutes?

Growing up in the 60's I had the unhappy privilege of experiencing the collapse of traditional Biblical morality in America. Schaeffer explained that this collapse had been in process, in the West, over several hundred years really, but it came to a head in the 1960's in the United States. Young people began to see clearly that the morality of their parents was foundationless. Their parents no longer knew why something was right or wrong, and certainly had no adequate explanation for their children. The foundations for such moral decisions had crumbled. When, as a culture, we stopped believing in the Bible and the God of the Bible, we lost any basis for determining what is right and what is wrong. Actually, the very words "right and wrong" lost any meaning. So why shouldn't we do promiscuous sex, drugs, alcohol, or anything else that felt good for the moment? Feeling good became the point and purpose of life. "If it feels good, do it!" Our parents demurred, but often the only reason they gave was something like "because that's the way it's always been", or "because its just wrong", or "decent people simply don't do that." Clearly, these kinds of answers were not enough. If tradition, or "just because", was the only reason for the kind of restraint and selflessness that morality called for, it simply wasn't sufficient.

Schaeffer postulated that there is a sufficient answer, one that squares with our experience of life. For example, most of us feel that love is good and hate is bad. And most of us suffer guilt if we do something wrong. Schaffer referenced one of my favorite writers, C.S. Lewis. Lewis in his book "Mere Christianity" illustrated how in the smallest matters of our lives, all of us accept some kind of standards of behavior that we expect everyone else to know about. Lewis wrote about that standard;

"...the moment anyone tells me I am not

keeping it, there starts up in my mind a string of excuses as long as your arm. The question at the moment is not whether they are good excuses. The point is that they are one more proof of how deeply, whether we like it or not, we believe in the Law of Nature. [Lewis' name for an implicit moral standard] Why else are we so anxious to make excuses for not having behaved decently?"

Yet, if we insist on denying God, and denying our person-ness, we must deny any moral standard. There simply can be no meaningful standard in an impersonal universe. So we cannot say that Hitler or Stalin or Idi Amin were wrong to kill millions and millions of people. We cannot say that there is anything wrong with our neighbor beating his wife, or with running a red light, or with the greed manifested on Wall Street. There is no reason we shouldn't lie, cheat, or steal, if it serves our purpose.

Here's the problem. Most of us human beings just can't live with that. Most of us, if we dig deep down inside, believe that some things are really right, and some things are really wrong. And as

Lewis explained, you don't have to scratch deeply at all to see this in the way people live. Just a few moments driving in traffic eloquently and infallibly proves our inclination to an angry assertion of right and wrong. There must be moral absolutes in play when cars meet at an intersection! When we squirm at being treated unfairly, or with a double standard, we are expressing a sense of innate morality that we assume is true for everyone. These expressions are part of the air we breathe, and they are common to all men and women everywhere. For instance murder, theft, lying and adultery, are almost universally looked upon as evil. Whether you're in a primitive culture, or a highly civilized culture, these moral inclinations are ubiquitous. One culture may say one wife at a time, and another may say several are ok, but both will assert that you may not simply take any woman you want.

Again, the impersonal, plus time, plus chance is not a feasible answer to this phenomenon. Just as personality can't arise from the impersonal, so common moral inclinations can't appear out of the blue. The only reasonable answer to this dilemma is that there is a real personal God, who is the standard for moral absolutes. And since we are created in His image, that sense of right and wrong is inherent, native, part of our genetic make-up.

As I sat in that auditorium night after night, I was gaining solid confidence in the personal, infinite, transcendent God of the Bible. I was seeing that the Bible and its God offered adequate and satisfactory answers to the basic, foundational questions of life. And believe it or not, Schaeffer really was able to give all this content in a week of lectures, and I hung on every word. After he was gone I went on to read and study his books, which only solidified in my mind what he had introduced me to that week. Schaeffer was able to thoroughly make clear to me that the only answers that adequately fit life and experience are the **answers that are found in the Judeo-Christian God**, the God revealed in the Old and New testaments, the God of my parents and grandparents.

Those several nights at my school changed the course of my life. They impacted my belief system in a way that allowed me to embrace my faith with real intellectual and philosophical integrity. They allowed me to continue in my faith, even at the darkest moments in my life, even when I was angry at God and was pushing Him away. Knowing that God is really there, even when, as you will see, I seriously do not like what he is doing, has kept me from jumping off a bridge! It has kept my times of deep discouragement from becoming times of unalterable despair. Do you remember the PBS television series "Anne of Green Gables?" Anne was having one of her signature emotional outbreaks, and she cried out to her guardian Marilla, "Don't you ever despair?" Marilla replied in her inimitable matter of fact way, "I do not. To despair is to turn your back on God."

I knew that I could not turn my back on God because I knew, I was convinced, that He is there, and that without Him life is utterly meaningless.

Now came the second and just as necessary part. I had to get to know this God, and I had to find out if he was enough to satisfy the needs, longings, and desires of my heart.

4 HUSBAND HUNTING

There is nothing quite like mornings in Southern California, and I loved them. Golden mornings, heavy with the scent of eucalyptus and jasmine. Arid mornings, with that wonderful warm dry air; air only slightly tainted by the marijuana haze rising from the hippie communes dotting the hillsides around my college dorm. I was attending a small college in the beautiful hills above Santa Barbara. My real purpose was to find a husband! I was crystal clear on this point. Leaving college without having secured a good man was tantamount to failure. I realize that in 2011, this sounds almost unbelievable, practically 18th century. Listen girls, this was 45 years ago, and I wanted to be married. I wanted a man, and I didn't even care if he was rich.

It was my junior year before I met the man who would become the love of my life. I was standing on the steps of the library my first day back, the first day of fall quarter. After summer vacation in Seattle I was soaking up the sunshine, breathing in the redolent air, feeling the sun warm and dry my bones. You know what Mark Twain said......the wettest coldest winter he ever spent was summer in Seattle. Or maybe he said San Francisco? Same difference. One of my friends bounded up the steps, gave me a big hug, and said "Have you met the new guy in choir?" Just that simply, Michael entered my life.

He was a Southern California boy, born into a family as polar opposite from mine as one could possibly conjure. His dad was in the entertainment industry, first as a TV news anchor, and then in advertising and production. Where we were allowed one TV show a week, the television set in Michael's house went on with the sunrise, and then turned to test pattern after everyone sitting in front of it had gone fast asleep. Where my parents were committed to each other for the long term, Mike's parents divorced when he was eight, and probably should have done so sooner. When we were still not allowed to go to movies, Rock Hudson was babysitting him. Really! We have the cutest picture of Mikey as a baby in Rock Hudson's arms. For those of you too young to know, Rock was a big movie star in the 50's and 60's.

While we attended church twice a Sunday, Mike quit believing in God when he found out there was no Santa Claus. While my family would read together, talk together, take vacations together, Mike was left pretty much on his own by a single mom just trying to survive. Where I was sure of being loved, Mike suffered from fear of abandonment, and from the greater fear of not being loved.

But we were enough alike to have confronted the same life questions. By the time Mike was eighteen, he was asking the same basic questions that I was, only from the other side of the coin. "Is this meaningless, absurd cycle really all there is to life?" "How did I get here, and does my being here have any significance?" "Is there a God, and if there is, how do I get to know him?"

God was just as eager to see Mike's questions answered as He had been with mine. So He brought a young man into his life his first year at Santa Barbara City College. Mike met Paul in English 101, and when they became good friends, Paul introduced him to the God of the Bible, and to Jesus Christ. Although he still had many questions, Mike knew he was on the right track. He encountered Francis Schaeffer about that same time, not in person, but through his books. And he found, as I had, answers to the questions that were so plaguing him. Michael had found Jesus, and he had found the answers to life's most basic questions, and he had also found his calling in life; sharing Jesus with others. So he left City College where he was a theatre arts major, to attend my college, planning on a pre-ministerial major.

Mike and I spent our junior year getting to know one another. I found him hilariously funny. He had what his professors at City College called phenomenal comedic timing. He could tell a joke like no one else. And he could, and still can, mimic any accent he heard, perfectly. French, British, Scottish, Indian, Chinese, to name a few. We started dating when I returned to campus for my senior year. This should be your first clue that he was not in a hurry with this relationship. He clearly did not subscribe to the "not married when graduated = failure" equation. When he asked me out to dinner for our first date, I totally did not know what to expect. Most of the guys in our class considered McDonalds a pretty good date. What should I wear? Casual, dressy, I had no idea, so I settled for a simple little black dress. Michael picked me up in front of my dorm, driving a 1964-½ mustang convertible. Even in 1970, these were considered very cool. I thought this was a very good sign. We drove into Santa Barbara, to a restaurant called "The Talk of the Town." I should mention one thing about the differences between Mike's and my families. Although my parents were pretty well off, when we went out to dinner we went to the Chinese restaurant in our neighborhood that my dad referred to as the "chink joint". I honestly did not know this was derogatory until Michael gave me a

43

severe reprimand when I used the term sometime after we were married. I thought it was the name of the restaurant! And I don't think my dad meant it derogatorily, it was that generational thing. Anyway, unless Dad announced when we sat down that "the sky's the limit", we were on a very tight leash when we ordered. Mike's mom and her new husband were not very well off, but lived like they were, so Michael would never have considered taking me to a less pricey place than "The Talk of the Town."

We sat at a lovely little table in front of a lovely little fireplace. There were fresh flowers on the table, and silver cutlery. I ordered fish, which the waiter brought out to me, quite dead, but uncooked, for my approval. I must have looked shocked, because Mike took over and assured the waiter that the fish was just fine. They certainly did not consider fish approval to be necessary at our family Chinese restaurant. We ate and talked, and talked some more, and after the main course Michael ordered us my first flaming dessert, served tableside. Crepes Suzette.

Dripping with butter and orange liqueur, they were heavenly. We sat at that table for hours, talking, sharing stories, sharing dreams, and I was caught, as my dad would say, hook, line, and sinker. I had always been quick to make decisions, and I knew I had found my husband. Now came the part about convincing him.

My senior year was flying by. I had been named to "Who's Who in American Colleges and Universities", and was on track to graduate Magna Cum Laude. The fact that I missed that honor by 1/10th of one grade point was completely Michael's fault. We had been dating steadily ever since that first magical dinner, and one of our favorite things to do was go out for coffee after his last class on Tuesday and Thursday afternoons. I did not see any reason to let him know that I still had a class to go to those afternoons; after all, my priorities were clear. Plus it was a completely irrelevant, one unit fetal pig lab that I had successfully avoided taking until the last quarter of my senior year. Why would I want anything to do with a fetal pig, and where were the animal rights activists anyway?! My advisor called me

45

into his office and advised me that, stunning GPA or not, I had to take this class in order to graduate. But coffee with Mike was a much higher priority. Fortunately my professor was a really good guy, who understood with clarity that a one unit fetal pig lab was not something that was going to impact my post college life one iota. The problem was that I was flunking the class because of a combination of never attending, and not doing the work. He came to me the last week of school, and made me a deal. If I would come to class and take the last test, he would give me the answers to that test, so that he could pass me with a grade of D, and I could graduate. Bless his heart, I took the deal, and there went my grade point average.

More to the point, I was graduating from college, and still single. Michael could not seem to step up to the plate if swinging meant committing to marriage. And could you blame him? His exposure to his parents' marriages had done nothing to convince him this was a road he was eager to travel. So, what now? Even though I had all the credentials to launch a career, that was not what I wanted. I was walking right into one of the pivotal periods of my life. Was I going to find that God met all the needs and desires of my life, even if I never married? Could God fill the hole that I was certain only a husband could? Was God enough for a single woman?

It would take almost a year living in Japan to find out.

5 ALONE WITH GOD

Excuse me? Japan? Yes, Japan. In September of 1971, I kissed Michael goodbye. He was headed south to start his new job as a youth pastor in a big church in Arizona. I boarded a 747 for the ten hour flight to Tokyo, Japan. I remember wondering as we winged further and further west, further and further from all that was loved and familiar, what in the world I was doing.

I had taken a job about 5000 miles across the ocean, in a small town in the north part of Japan's main island, teaching English to college students and businessmen. In Japan in those days only native Japanese were allowed to teach English in public schools. The result of this policy was that although every student had something like five years of mandatory English lessons, they could not understand a word any average American said to them. And the American was just as unable to understand a word of the English being spoken to him. Just imagine having one Japanese person who had never heard English spoken, teach another Japanese person how to pronounce an English word, like "little", or "ready", or any word actually, and you quickly grasp the problem. It was a quintessential example of the blind leading the blind. So there were ready jobs for American English speaking persons to teach classes in foreign language schools and businesses in what was called "Conversational English."

I arrived in Tokyo in September of 1971. Back then, Japan was a land of contrasts. It had a veneer of Westernization, but the slightest scratch revealed centuries and centuries of imbedded tradition. It was a land of unbelievable beauty, both in nature and the arts, but with a blatant cruelty and pornography evidenced everywhere.

And it had awful weather that time of year. It was hot, sticky, and humid. The gentleman deplaning in front of me fell to the tarmac in an epileptic fit. I wondered if it was an omen. Everything was strange. There was blatant and disturbing pornography on the billboards. The din of honking horns and blaring sirens was deafening. Taking a taxi was tantamount to taking your life in your hands. And it was crowded. You could not walk without being jostled first on one side, and then on the other, by the crowds surrounding you. To an American like me, everyone looked alike. There was none of the melting pot influence I was so used to at home. It made putting names and faces together really difficult, and I found myself searching for any distinguishing feature to help me out. I lapsed into high school German as my mind made desperate attempts to understand and speak Japanese.

Restaurants posted their menus by displaying plastic versions of every dish they offered in a box window that you could peruse from the street. I was very hungry for anything familiar, so when I saw what appeared to be an ice cream sundae with chocolate sauce on top, I went straight inside and managed to make clear to the waiter that I would like to order one. I cannot emphasize enough my disgust when I discovered with my first bite that the "chocolate sauce" was actually bean paste. Yuck!

From Tokyo I took the train to Sendai, about 250 miles north, where I was contracted with a foreign language school to teach English. I arrived in Sendai in the middle of a monsoon. The rain was falling in impenetrable sheets that drenched you to the skin in about two seconds. My body clock was in shock. Sendai time was 16 hours ahead of Seattle time. So when it was bedtime in Sendai, my body was ready to wake up and get going. And about mid morning in Sendai I was totally ready for bed.

For the first time in my life I was alone. All my familiar props and crutches were gone. My family was at home in Seattle. Mike was settling into his new job in Arizona. I did not have a single friend. I did not have a church family. I was a foreigner in a foreign land. And there were not very many foreigners in that part of Japan at that time. I would walk down the street, and some little black-haired child coming toward me would stop in her tracks, point a shaking finger at me, and scream at the top of her voice "Gaijin!" That means foreigner, or foreign devil, or alien, or something like that....definitely not a polite term for someone not a native. Even for me it was a bit unnerving, particularly as half the city would turn to look.

God had me exactly where he wanted me.

I would lie in bed in the middle of the night, wide awake, and He was there, waiting for me to talk to him. "Am I enough for you? Can you be happy with just me - the God of the Universe, who created you and loves you, and has a plan for you? Can you trust me, even if it means that you are not going to marry Mike, even if it means that you will never marry anyone? Even if it means that you are going to live here in Japan teaching English for the rest of your life? Is it enough to walk hand in hand with the one true God? Will you choose me first, over any other?" The basic issue that God was addressing had to do with idols. Idols are anything in life that is more important than Him. These idols do not have to be little stone statues that I burn candles in front of. In fact, those would be really obvious, very external. I could easily say "I don't have any idols. Look! Do you see any little statues?" But the idols God wanted to address in my life were the invisible ones, the insidious ones, the ones that were in themselves not bad. They were only idols if I held them wrongly. Things like wanting to be married. Wanting to be financially secure. Wanting to have life be easy, and happy, and meaningful. These are all good things to want. But at the point where they become little saviors - where I look to a husband to save me from my loneliness, or to money to save me from my insecurity, or to friends to save me from feeling insignificant - they become an idol. And God hates idols. Not because He is the great kill-joy in the sky. Not because He is the celestial Scrooge bah-humbugging at everybody. But He hates idols because He knows, since he made us, what it takes to make us happy. Really happy. He hates idols because He loves us and knows it is only as we relate to Him, and make that relationship the primary one in our lives, that we will find life to be the beautiful, scary, mind boggling, exuberant experience it can be.

As I was sorting this issue, I found the book of Hosea in the Bible. Hosea was a prophet to the people of Israel at a time in their history when they had abandoned God and gone after other idols. One of their favorites was Baal, the fertility God of the Canaanites. The Israelites had entered into all kinds of sin in the worship of this god, including homicide, perjury, theft, and sexual sin. The message of Hosea was of God's unending love for these people who had chosen to walk away from Him. God had Hosea illustrate how much God loved His people with Hosea's own life. He told Hosea to marry a woman who was a prostitute, a woman of very bad reputation. God wanted to show Israel that He loved them as a man loves his wife. At one point Gomer, Hosea's wife, left him and went to live with another man. When that man tired of her, Hosea had to give him money to buy his wife back. Hosea's grief and pain over his wayward wife gives us insight into how God, in his love and faithfulness, feels toward us when we stray from Him to serve idols. The Book of Hosea shows how God loves me, and all his people, illustrated by the relationship between Hosea and Gomer. Hosea chapter 6 says;

> "Come, let us return to the Lord. He has torn us to pieces, but he will heal us, He has injured us, but he will bind up our wounds. After two days he will revive us; on the third day He will restore us, that we may live in his presence. Let us acknowledge the Lord; let us press on to acknowledge Him. As surely as the sun rises He will appear; He will come to us like the winter rains, like the spring rains that water the earth." (v.1-3)

Those words gripped me as I read them on those long, wide-awake nights. It seemed like bringing me to Japan *was* tearing me to pieces; that removing me from all that was familiar and comfortable *was* injuring me. But God was using the time alone with me to confront my idols, and then to heal me, bind up my wounds, and restore me so that I could start to learn to live in His presence.

Eventually, I started agreeing with God that He could be in control of my life, not me. I agreed with Him that just knowing Him was enough to infuse my life with joy and meaning and purpose. I agreed with God that I would stay in Japan as long as He wanted me to. I wasn't necessarily overjoyed about this prospect, but I was learning that clinging to God did fill the holes I felt inside. I was learning that trying to fill those holes with travel, or with a man, or with money, or with friends, did not work. Nothing was satisfying like Jesus.

Even though I was very lonely, I was settling in a bit to my new life. I enjoyed my students, and loved going out to dinner and drinks with them. Sake is the iconic Japanese alcoholic drink, and it seemed to have a magical effect on my students. After just one glass they would become significantly more relaxed and less self-conscious.

Amazingly this would improve their English speaking skills by at least 100%!

But I was still a foreigner in a foreign land, and was looking for anything to provide a modicum of familiarity and comfort. Like American style toilets. Japanese toilets were absolute Greek to a foreigner like me. They were just a hole in the ground. They were definitely easier for men than women to navigate; no surprise in this male dominated society. But to my relief, someone told me there was a Western style toilet in the big hotel in the middle of town. Sure enough, on the 5th floor, there it was in all it's welcome glory. A shiny white, porcelain, honest-to-goodness, sit-on, real, flushing, American-style toilet! So, my morning routine became; teach an hour class at the foreign language school, walk a few blocks to the big hotel, take the elevator to the 5th floor, use the American toilet, go back down and out the door to my next class of Japanese executives.

Did I mention there were not very many Americans in Sendai? It did not take long for the doorman at the hotel to figure out where I was going at 10:30 every morning, and what I was doing. Pretty soon, as I approached the hotel doors, a smiling doorman would greet me. "Good morning, Sensei." Sensei was the Japanese honorable word for teacher. He would grin knowingly as he walked me to the elevator and pushed the button for the 5th floor. "Have a good day Sensei," he would say as he greeted my descending elevator and walked me out the front door to the street.

It got to be Christmas time, and I was miserable. I missed Mike, I missed my family, and I missed all the familiar Christmas celebrations. Christmas morning I was going to take the train a couple of hours south to have Christmas dinner with an American missionary family. It was freezing cold and I was feeling very sorry for myself. The train stations in Japan had some really great food vendors. My favorite was the soba stand where I could get a steaming bowl of soba noodles, in a wonderful broth, topped with crispy tender delicious tempura shrimp. This cost me 80 yen which was then the equivalent of about 25 cents American.

I particularly liked the fact that it was completely acceptable to make grossly loud slurping noises as you used your chopsticks to get the noodles from the bowl to your mouth. It was a very efficient way of eating. You got the chopsticks around the first bunch of noodles, and then just kept noisily sucking, using the chopsticks to keep a steady stream of noodles coming. Standing at the soba bar, surrounded by happily slurping Japanese, was when I felt most at home. I tried to bring this sloppy but happy way of eating home to the States with me. But the first time I sat down to a plate of pasta with Mike, pulled out my chopsticks, and starting shoveling and slurping, he looked at me absolutely aghast. Talking to him now, he says he remembers this very vividly. His response to what he considered an unforgivable breach of table manners was something like "What the hell?!" I tried to explain that this was perfectly acceptable in Japan. He was adamant that this was not Japan, that this was America, and he considered such dinner table behavior completely unacceptable. Kill joy. I was sorely tempted to stick my tongue out at him.

Anyway, this was Christmas morning in Japan and I was going to treat myself to the most expensive Bento box at the station. If you've been to a Japanese restaurant here in the USA, you've probably had a Bento box of some sort. It usually consists of little tidbits of various yummy Japanese foods like rice, tempura, teriyaki chicken, probably some sushi. Well, my Japanese was not good enough to decipher what was in this pricey little Bento box. But it was going to be my Christmas treat, so I bought it and on to the train I went. Once settled in and racing down the track, I opened my Christmas meal. There, glaring at me with a malevolent stare, was an eel. A complete eel, head and all. A dead, definitely raw, as in not in any way exposed to a heat source, eel. It was cut into two long pieces, with a very "how dare you do this to me you despicable person" look in his eye that must have been there when he was unceremoniously dispatched and attached to my Bento box. That Bento box was pretty much emblematic of my Christmas. I spent the balance of the two hour train ride contemplating again what the heck I was doing there. But I knew what I was doing there. I was learning that God, and God alone, was enough.

Wouldn't it be marvelous if I only had to have this kind of experience once, and for the rest of my life I would never stray, never reach out for idols, never forget that God is enough? Marvelous, but not likely. As you will see, and as the great 19th century preacher Charles Spurgeon used to say, we get filled up with this sure knowledge of God, but we tend to leak.

On Valentines Day I went to my mail box in Sendai, and there was a Valentines Day card from Mike. He asked me to marry him. (Finally! It certainly took him long enough! I should have learned from that experience what it has taken me 38 years to figure out – my husband is very slow to make decisions.) In a phone call that cost me 76,000 yen, I said yes. I was not going to trust the mail to get this answer to him. And since it was rather difficult to facilitate an American wedding from Japan, in early April I was on my way back to Seattle, planning for August nuptials.

I look back now and even though, as you will see, God has had to keep reminding me and teaching me that only He is sufficient to meet all my needs, I know that the foundations of the success of my marriage were laid in Japan. There I began to learn that nobody, not even a beloved husband, could meet the basic needs of my heart. Because I had begun to understand that Mike could not be God to me, because I did not expect him to be the source of meaning and joy in my life, because I knew there was a God who loved me as no one else could, I was free to love Mike without putting unrealistic expectations on him. At least most of the time!

6 REAL SATISFACTION

A few months before we got married, Mike took a job as a youth pastor in a church east of Seattle. So we started our life together in a little tiny Victorian rental house on the shores of Lake Washington. It was drafty, with old single pane windows that rattled and shook with every gust of wind. It was cold enough in the master bedroom to hang meat. But it had a lovely bay window, and a primrose lined front walk, and we loved it. I had begun to discover that, like my grandmother before me, I was a gifted interior designer, and I loved to practice on our houses. I could visualize just the perfect window treatment in that bay window; individual sunny yellow roller shades, with scalloped hems trimmed with fringe, and creamy side panels tied back to frame the view. Mike could see it too, so we set to work, first sewing the side panels. Then we found just the perfect roller shades at our local Sears. These 40 years later, I remember with undiminished clarity the moment we finished installing the blinds and panels. We stood back to admire our work. They were, indeed, perfect. They beautifully framed the view out the window, and brought color and light to the room. They looked exactly as I had envisioned. I stood there looking at them, thinking they were exactly what I wanted. But I realized acutely that deep inside they did exactly nothing to address the basic longings of my life. They did nothing, nada, zip, to make me any happier, or more fulfilled, or more satisfied than I already was. It was a defining moment for me. A moment when I really understood *emotionally*, not just intellectually, that nothing satisfies like Jesus. The old hymn became a life statement for me.

"I'd rather have Jesus than silver or gold.
I'd rather have Jesus than riches untold.
I'd rather have Jesus than houses or land.
I'd rather be held by his nail pierced hand.
Than to be the king of a vast domain, and be held in sin's dread sway.

I'd rather have Jesus than anything this world affords today."

This doesn't mean that I gave up on interior design. Not at all. I love creating warm, hospitable, inviting, cozy spaces that make people feel like they want to come in and put their feet up. It doesn't mean that I didn't enjoy my beautiful window treatments. And it doesn't mean that I don't love beautiful things. It does mean that I don't hold on to those things too tightly, and that usually I am able to maintain perspective. While comfortable and beautiful homes are a good thing, and creating them is how I make my living, they are not what is ultimately important in life. And they are not what will satisfy the longings of my soul. If I had not been in relationship with Jesus when those window treatments went up in my first home, when I stood back and looked at them, and realized that they did NOT satisfy my soul, what would I have done? Probably what so many of us in this culture do....go for bigger and better window treatments - or cell phones, or cars, or houses, or marriages, or, or, or... If I just tweak this here, or add another layer there, or change the color of the fringe, then I'll be happy.   But of course, the changes are no more satisfying than the original, because the hole in my heart is God shaped, and only He can fill it.

7 MIRACLE BABIES

We had been married two years and were ready to start a family. Now you are probably thinking, "Ok, here's another opportunity to see if God is enough." And you are right. Try as we might, I could not get pregnant. My OB-GYN ran every possible test, on both of us, and after three years of miserable test after miserable test, he finally looked me in the eye and said "You are not able to have children."

I was devastated. I was angry. I was distraught. Was God punishing me? Did he not care about my desire to have children? Everywhere I looked in the Bible being "barren" was something that reflected negatively on one's womanhood. And well meaning friends and acquaintances did not help. They started commenting on why we weren't having children. "Hey, when are you guys going to settle down and have kids?" "What's the matter with you, don't you like babies?" Amazing, isn't it, how unbelievably cruel people can be, even when they surely don't mean to be. "Just tell them the truth," Mikey would say. "Tell them that you are unable to have children and that will shut them up." But I found those words almost impossible to get out of my mouth.

It was like my Japan experience all over again. Is God enough to satisfy the longings of my soul, even if I never have children? I mean this is different than window treatments. This is *children* we are talking about. But I was learning. I knew in my mind that He was enough, and my heart was slowly following.

Then a friend of ours told us about an adoption agency in Seattle. "Go see Hegge," he said. "He can help you adopt a baby." So we made an appointment, and a couple of weeks later we were sitting in Hegge's office. "What do you want?" he asked. We weren't fussy. We wanted a blond haired, blue eyed, baby boy. "Well," he said, "that could take years." He went on. "I think," he said, "that God wants you to have your own children." Just great, I thought.

Out loud I said "I am not able to have children." There, I had said it. Hegge looked at me, and his face was full of compassion and understanding. "I know," he said, "but with your permission I am going to pray right now for you that God will give you your own child, because I think that is what God is saying to me. And when you feel emotionally ready, I want you to come back, and my whole staff will pray for you to get pregnant." I thought the likelihood of my ever being ready for the whole staff to pray for me was slim, but Hegge prayed with us, and sent us on our way. "Come back in a couple of weeks," he said.

In a couple of weeks, I came down with a bad case of the flu. I was vomiting morning, noon, and night. I couldn't keep anything on my stomach. This went on for almost two months before my dad and my husband joined forces and insisted I go the doctor. So I went to our old family practitioner. He checked me over pretty thoroughly, and then said there did not seem to be anything wrong with me. "I think you are pregnant," he said. "Can't be" I replied. "I am not able to have children." He suggested that it couldn't hurt to run a pregnancy test anyway, so I peed in a cup, and we went home. This was in 1978, when it took hours for the results of a pregnancy test. I was still vomiting when the phone rang. It was the Doctor. "You are pregnant," he said. I must have hung up, because he called back about ten minutes later and started over again. "You are pregnant," he said. I was not believing him. So I called my OB-GYN. I told the nurse that my family doctor told me I was pregnant. I could hear the deep concern in her voice. "You get in here right now," she said, and we did.

When Mike and I got into the consulting room, my doctor, who was really a caring and wonderful guy, tried to gently tell me that there were all kinds of reasons that a family doctor might think I was pregnant, but we were going to get to the bottom of what was really wrong with me. I lay back on the gurney, and he began to gently poke around. The more he poked, the stranger the look on his face got.   Finally he pulled out the instrument they use to hear heart beats in the womb. He slid that around for a while. Then he took it off and looked at me. "There's a heart beat in there," he said. "There's a baby in there," he said. "It's a miracle," he said. And we all started to cry.

I was two and a half months pregnant.

All I have to say is, watch what you wish for. I was sicker than a dog the whole nine months. They gave me a drug to help stop the vomiting, but all it really did was make me too tired to actually throw up. I was just as nauseated. By my ninth month, my blood pressure was off the charts, I was highly toxic, and it was time to get that baby out. An emergency C-section produced a beautiful blond haired, blue-eyed, baby boy. We named him Jeddidiah, which means "Beloved of the Lord". It was God's name for Solomon. The really great thing is that I woke up the next morning, and for the first time in nine months, I wasn't vomiting.

Jedd was, and still is, an absolute delight.

And I know God has something special in mind for Jedd, because two years later, He quite literally saved his life. We were on vacation in California visiting family and friends. We had just finished lunch, and were getting in the car to head further south. We were driving a miniscule sub compact. Jedd's car seat was tucked into the back seat behind the driver, and I had made him a little bed in the portion of the hatchback behind the passenger seat. It was nap time, and he was tired and fussy, so Mike started to tuck him into the little bed. I am not exaggerating when I say that a voice from heaven said to me "Put him in his car seat." I turned to Mike and said "We have to put him in his car seat." Mike didn't look at me funny, he didn't question me, he just put Jedd in his car seat. Five minutes later, out on the freeway, we came to a stop behind a long line of cars. The gentleman behind us in a Toyota Celica stopped. A young woman behind him was driving her mom and brother home in her huge old 1960's era station wagon. It might as well have been an armored tank. It was her 17th birthday. She came around the bend going 65 MPH, saw the stopped cars, took her hands off the wheel, and started screaming. She hit the car behind us at full speed, that car was thrown on top of her station wagon, and they both hit us, slamming us into the car in front of us. The passenger side of the car where Jedd would have been sleeping was wiped out. Our car was totaled. Jedd got a few cuts and bruises from his car seat being thrown into the seat in front of him. Both Mike and I limped away, bruised and sore. Even though this proved to be a major source of his eventual back issues, we were ok. The gentleman behind us had to be extricated from his car with the jaws of life. The young woman and her family were taken away in ambulances. Since we were the least hurt, we got to spend an hour and a half on the freeway with sirens screaming, and emergency vehicles coming and going, and thousands of cars creeping by, staring as they went. Jedd was howling at the top of his lungs, but he was alive and well. God had reached down from heaven and saved his life.

When Jedd was two and a half, the memory of being pregnant had faded enough that we decided to try for another baby. "There's nothing like getting pregnant once to solve the not being able to get pregnant problem," my doctor said. Sure enough, in two weeks I woke up vomiting. "It's certain to not be as bad this time," the doctor said. Two months, three months, four months, still vomiting. At five months, I was still vomiting, but now started bleeding as well. Into the hospital I went, not to the maternity ward, but to the women's surgical ward, never a positive sign. The ultrasound showed that I had another beautiful baby boy. And...a total placenta previa.

A placenta previa is where the placenta, rather than attaching to the side of the uterine wall where it is supposed to attach, attaches to the bottom of the uterus, on the cervix. This means that as the baby grows he exerts more and more pressure on the placenta, causing it to tear, which is why I was bleeding. It is also impossible to get the baby out vaginally. A very kindly nurse came into my room and told me to prepare myself for losing this child. Total placenta previa babies never make it to full term, she said. Even if the tear in my placenta healed, it was bound to happen again. When Dr. Graham came in I told him through tears what she had said. He left the room for a few minutes. I never saw that nurse again. When he came back he told me that if I did exactly what he said, this baby was going to make it. What I had to do was go to bed, and stay there. I could get up to go to the bathroom, and that was it. I had to have someone with me 24/7, because if the placenta broke I only had 45 minutes before the baby and I would both be dead.

We did exactly as instructed. It was really fine with me. I generally don't suffer from guilt, and I enjoyed being waited on hand and foot. Jedd would curl up in the bed with me and read books. I finished crocheting the baby blanket I had started but never finished before Jedd was born. I read all the books I wanted to read. Poor Mikey, life was much harder for him. He was now pastoring a little church in Kirkland, a suburb of Seattle. But not only was he being a pastor, he was being full time mom, full time dad, and chief cook and bottle washer. Dear friends from our church brought in meals to help him out almost every night for about three months. What an amazing manifestation of grace and love and care that was. We will never forget it. My mom and dad were there to help every minute they could, but by the time the baby was ready to be born Mike was exhausted. Tyler - that was our baby's name - could not emerge soon enough.

They planned to deliver Tyler a month early, as they did not want to risk the pressure on the placenta that would increase every day that Tyler continued to grow. "I am free on December 24th," Dr. Graham said. I thought of my son having a Christmas Eve birthday, and we settled on December 29 instead. It would be another C-section of course, only this time they had to cut through the pumping placenta to get to the baby. I lost so much blood that I stopped vomiting, and passed out. Mike, who was there with me, said that the blood spurted out and splashed all over the floor. But Tyler was born. He looked like a wizened little old man. His skin hung on him in folds because he had actually lost weight the last month in the womb as the placenta stopped nourishing him. But he had my grandmother's dark skin and dark hair. He was absolutely gorgeous.

It was 1981, and AIDS was still off the radar of most doctors. I had lost a lot of blood, and needed a transfusion. My doctor came to see me the morning after Tyler was born. "You know," he said, "you lost a lot of blood, and normally we would do a transfusion. But," he said, "I'm really not comfortable with that. It is going to take you a year to replenish your own blood, but I think that is what we should do." Uncharacteristically, I did not question him or argue. So that's what we did. It took me a year to fully regain my strength and stamina. But my doctor knew enough then, even though he didn't explain it to me, to be suspicious of contamination in the blood supply. It wasn't until years later when all the news started breaking about the women who contracted AIDS in the early eighties from blood transfusions after child birth, that I understood the significance of that decision.

God was continuing to reach down and touch our life with miracles. And He had blessed us with two precious little boys, each of whom was in his own way a miracle baby. But it did not necessarily follow that these children would be little angels. They would be a challenge to parent, a challenge made more daunting by the titanic difference between how Mike and I had been parented. Like the iceberg that sank the Titanic, parenting almost sank us.

8 THE SINS OF THE FATHERS

It says in the Bible that God "visits the sins of the fathers on the children and on the grandchildren to the third and fourth generation." My experience with my husband has convinced me that nowhere is that more true than in fathering. Mike's dad was quite simply an abusive, awful father. Actually, there was nothing simple about it. He was the most manipulative, slippery, selfish man I had ever met. He was quick to tell Mike that he loved him, but even quicker to show that the only one he really loved was himself. The credibility gap between his words and his actions was cavernous. Mike would say carnivorous. Emotional and verbal abuse were his trademarks. Because Mike's mom was equally a victim of his father's abuse, she was not able to protect Mike, to stand up for him, or even to help him sort the process. He was abused by his dad, and then abandoned physically by him, and he was abandoned emotionally by his mom.

In his dad's defense, Mike's grandfather was even worse than his dad. Mike remembers his grandfather as a stern, nasty, hateful person, who, if he felt any love for his son or grandson at all, certainly never let on that he did. Mike's dad left home at a very early age to escape his father, but he didn't escape the heritage. He lied to Mike, manipulated him, made promises he never kept, and methodically and mercilessly, even if unintentionally, destroyed any sense Mike had that he was worthy of being loved.

I remember one day shortly after we were married. The phone rang. It was Mike's dad. I handed him the phone and then watched in dismay as my husband changed in front of me. He went from the man I knew to someone I did not recognize. He was like a whipped puppy. It was like he was trying to find a footing on a steep slope covered in small, smooth pebbles. He was trying to say something, respond somehow, in a way that would please his dad. When he finally hung up the phone he stormed out of the house without a word to me. He was gone for about an hour. A long walk was his way to expel the anger and hurt and frustration that talking to his dad had brought on. I could have happily stuck a stake in my father-in-law's heart.

I would love to leave this all out, to cover this aspect of our lives with the cone of silence, especially as it is very important to Mike that he honor his father and his mother, even now. And it is very important to me that I honor my husband. But we both agree that this story cannot be truthfully told any other way. God cannot really be enough if He is not enough in the most difficult and painful experiences of life. And the most painful reality in our marriage was that Mike became a very angry father. But not without reason!

His childhood was so different than mine that it was almost impossible for me to grasp. Plus I didn't understand why my deep and passionate love for him was not enough to make up for his past. I'd say really stupid things like "Can't you just get over it? After all, look at the way I love you!" One time when I started down this road Mike picked up an antique dining chair and threw it - quite literally - down the basement stairs. Then he went after it, picked it up and proceeded to thrash it to pieces on the concrete floor. My inability to "get it" was rubbing salt in his wounds.

But he did know how much I cherished him, so bit by bit, year by year, he began to open up to me about his dad. He told me about one time when he was about four years old. His dad took him to the rodeo. Mikey was so excited! He was actually more excited about doing something special with his dad than he was about the rodeo. But when they got there, his dad locked him in the car in the parking lot, and went in alone. (You can imagine my sky rocketing blood pressure as he is telling me this....) Mike had no idea what he had done wrong, or why he was being punished. Years later he came to wonder if he had provided the cover story for his dad to accomplish one of his many sexual dalliances.

It was after one of these episodes that his mom finally pulled herself together enough to throw his dad out. After the divorce, Mike saw his dad only infrequently. But one summer when he was fourteen his dad invited him to spend two months with him in New York City where he was living with his new wife. Mike was so excited! Ok, so he's a slow learner. Or maybe "hope springs eternal." No sooner did he arrive in New York then his dad left for a six week business Trip.

When Mike approached his college graduation his dad promised to take him on a trip to Mexico as a graduation present, just as he had with his older brother. Instead, after graduation, his Dad handed him his present - a tape recorder - and said "Don't you lose it!"   On his way up to Seattle to see me, Mike's car was broken into and the tape recorder was stolen. I began to see that there might be major issues when Mike was so afraid his dad would find out it had been stolen that he took every cent he had and bought a new identical tape recorder, never telling his dad what had happened.

My husband is quick to tell me that I do not have to make excuses for him. He has come to grips with his fathering, has confessed his sins to our sons, and has sought and won their forgiveness. I am not excusing him, but I do have to tell the whole story. Without the facts of his childhood the story would be dreadfully incomplete.

There were factors other than Mike's anger that fed our parenting issues. A critical one was the difference between how our parents viewed children. For Mike's parents, children were there to serve their needs. His Dad would produce Mike when he wanted to show off his son's comic talent and acting ability. Mike was always expected to remember his dad's birthday and Christmas, although his dad was often too busy to reciprocate. When Mike asked once if he could borrow some money for two weeks, his dad replied, "Ok, but if you don't pay it back I will kill you." And Mike was pretty sure he meant it.

On the other hand, my parents felt it was their mission to serve their children. I was lavished with love. I was made to feel special and worthy and important. They spent time with us around the dinner table, and on long walks. Dad took me to "Gone With The Wind" when surely he would have loved to do almost anything else. They planned and executed family vacations. When we occasionally asked my parents for a loan, their response was "How much do you need?" After our boys came, when I would suggest to Mike that we take them camping, or on some similar family outing, he would look at me blankly. Then he would agree that it was a very good idea. But he would bemoan the fact that he had not thought of it himself. It was outside of his realm of experience of family.

Do you begin to grasp the chasm between Mike's childhood experiences, and mine, and perhaps understand the potential impact of that chasm? My innate confidence and the way I was parented, combined with Mike's insecurities and the way he was parented, kept us at loggerheads when it came to parenting our boys. We clung to each other, treasured each other, honored each other, reveled in each other, in every other area of our lives. But when it came to Jedd and Tyler, how to discipline them, what constituted disrespect, how to respond to dirty rooms, how to handle the rebellion they exhibited, we were on different planets. And there is no question that our boys were rebellious, and were starting to make some bad choices. They were after all, assured and confident like me, and were not loathe to defy us.

Take tattoos for instance. "Mom", Jedd asked when he was about sixteen, "May I get a tattoo?" My response was instantaneous. "Absolutely not." On this point Mike and I were, amazingly, in absolute agreement. "But its *art*, Mom!" I was not buying it. Both his Dad and I expressly and with no lack of clarity forbade Jedd to get a tattoo. It must have been about a week later when he came home with a bulldog tattoo, permanently (but thank God not eternally) embedded on his arm. An obscene number of tattoos followed. Tyler was equally rebellious, although he exhibited it differently.

Mike's and my tolerance level for this kind of behavior was totally different. Rightly or wrongly,

I expected rebellion from my boys. After all, I knew my own heart and the rebellion that I was capable of, even though for the most part I had not succumbed to it. But Mike did not expect it, which made it all the more difficult for him. In spite of the dreadful parenting he had received - or maybe because of it - he had chosen to be obedient, even dutiful. He had been your basic really good kid. So it did nothing for his anger issues that our sons, who had the benefit of two loving and committed parents, were so often choosing disobedience and rebellion. In fact, their behavior aggravated the deep seated anger Mike felt toward his dad, which in turn contributed to making him an angry father.

People are so complex, so multi-faceted, so broken. My sweetheart of a husband could be a sweetheart of a father, but he could also be the complete opposite. He was a gifted, loving, compassionate, friend and pastor. Everyone who encountered him saw Jesus in him, but his own sons saw a very angry man. "He was such a hypocrite!" you might say. Well, yes. Aren't we all! We are all sinners, needy and broken, and desperate for the redemption that only Jesus offers. And even when we claim that redemption and begin clinging to Jesus, our brokenness, our sins, still linger. At best, they sneak along the edges of our lives like a thorn covered blackberry vine, prickly and seemingly indestructible. Then at the worst possible moment they wind around our feet, sending us crashing face first into the pavement of life.

It's not that we didn't have wonderful family times together. We absolutely did. We attended all the boys' baseball, basketball, and football games, and we took them to Disneyland. All four of us would laugh uproariously together. Jedd and Tyler were their father's sons, and they could match him accent for accent, and joke for joke. But that did not keep them from bearing the brunt of his anger when they were rebellious or disrespectful or irresponsible, or sometimes, just being boys.

"How did your marriage survive this?" you might ask. I had learned in a profound and intense way in Japan that only God was enough to satisfy the deepest longings of my heart. So it followed that I did not expect Mike to be God. Since he wasn't God, I was not surprised by his flaws. Dismayed, but not surprised. Nor was I going to give up on him because of them, even though they were not insignificant. They caused distress, disruption and grief in our family. I should add that my husband could probably pen quite a treatise on what it is like to be married to someone like me who is just as flawed, only differently.

Was God enough in this experience in our marriage and our family? Absolutely. God was there, in our lives, actively at work to accomplish healing, forgiveness, wholeness for Mike, even though it would take years and is still happening.

There were times when Mike, acutely aware of his anger, would despair of ever changing. There were times when he would weep over his failures as a Dad, and wonder if there was any hope for him. But God brought into his life a faithful friend and mentor named Gib who would remind him of what Gib called the "doctrine of process."

It's a truth that articulates the main idea of this book - that God is enough.   God is enough because in the face of our sins and brokenness He keeps working with us and shaping us to be the person we really want to be. He never gives up on us. God is enough because in His skillful hands the sin-caused pain and trials of our lives are part of the very process that transforms us. God is enough because he never despairs of us, so we need never despair of ourselves. God is enough because even when we're at our worst, He sees us as precious and valuable. God is enough because he doesn't accuse us but helps us face our sins squarely, and forgives us. And God is enough because he brings a friend like Gib, or a book, or a chapter from the Bible, or the beauty of His creation to remind us of his transforming love, and that we're all "in process." The Apostle Paul expressed his confidence in a God of process in Philippians 1.6 "...being confident of this, that He who began a good work in you will carry it on to completion until the day of Christ Jesus." That has become one of my husband's favorite verses because of what it reveals about God's love for him in the midst of his failures and flaws. Because of how God loved us, and because of our deep and abiding love for each other, we could continue to walk together through the parenting discord we were experiencing.

9 THE DEATH OF OUR CHURCH

You may have heard of the question proverbially posed to Abraham Lincoln's wife after his assassination. "Other than that, Mrs. Lincoln, how was the play?" Our life was like that. Other than our parenting issues, we were happy and content.

But like so many families in the 1980's we found that a second income was necessary to make ends meet, so I went back to design school to augment my natural talent with skills like furniture design and construction, how to read architectural drawings, space planning and scaled floor plans. I started my own interior design business and named it "Your Place Interiors". I wanted the name of my business to underscore my commitment to helping people express their personal story in their homes, as my home expressed our personal taste, and our family story.

We reveled in cooking, and in having people over for dinner. Hospitality was something both Mike and I loved. And we extended that hospitality to friends and neighbors, as well as to those who could not reciprocate. We opened our home to young men, some troubled, some not, giving them a place to safely live, and safely ask their questions. I remember late one night when Mike and I both woke up to the sounds of one of these young men vomiting in our living room. We looked at each other and grinned wryly. Both of us instantly thought of Francis Schaeffer's lectures on Christians and love. "Don't talk about love until you have drunks vomiting on your carpet!" he had said. We felt like he would have been proud.

One time one of the guys living with us stole our car. We went to bed with a car, and woke up without one. The cops found the car, and the young man, and brought them both back to us. Mike and he had a long talk, and when we found pornography in his bedroom, he was invited to find a new place to live. We did have our young sons to consider. But God was teaching us, and we were learning, that the people he brought into our lives to serve were more important than our stuff, whether it was our carpet, or our car.

After buying, selling, building, and selling a couple of times, we designed and built our dream house on an old apple orchard in the waterfront town of Kirkland. It had lots of dentil moldings and trim. It was painted pink and had a turquoise door. We called it a "faux Georgian" because of it's traditional details and architecture. We loved it. It was the kind of house that people driving by slowed down to admire. My kitchen had a fireplace and a bay window. My office was off the kitchen so that I could work at home when the boys got home from school.

And the little church that Mike was pastoring was an absolute delight to us. We had started with just a few families, and met in one of their homes. Having a home church had some wonderful advantages. After Sunday service, everyone would go back to their cars and pull out a casserole, or a salad, or a dessert, and we would all have Sunday dinner together. My siblings were spread all over the country, so the boys had no aunts or uncles or cousins nearby. The families in our church became that extended family to them. The church children were in the same age range as our boys, so Jedd and Tyler's best friends were their church friends. The adults in our church were second parents to them. Even though the church never got very large, we did out-grow meeting in a home. But meeting in a school did nothing to diminish the sense of family and community. We took seriously Jesus' admonition to love one another. We were involved positively in each others' lives. These were the people, after all, who so faithfully and graciously brought us meals for all those months that I spent in bed while pregnant with Tyler. If you became part of our church you weren't a stranger for long. You were embraced, befriended, included. And Michael is a fine preacher, one of the very best I have ever heard. His communication gifts combined with his faith, and hours of study, made his sermons compelling, interesting, and meaningful, even though they were usually almost an hour long!

But it wasn't all sweetness and light. Community is a wonderful but fragile thing. Love among friends can be real and substantial, but it can so easily be damaged and even destroyed. And there are many forces at work to bring about that damage. Misunderstandings, offenses, wounds, and judgments are part and parcel of fallen human currency. And Christians are not exempted from this human brokenness. The potential for reconciliation and healing among damaged relationships is powerfully available through Jesus, but too often we Christians squander that potential. And our church was going to do just that.

The sad truth is that pastors' and their families are subject to a great deal of scrutiny. Ours was no different. So, although Mike was a loving, committed, compassionate, and gifted pastor, our parenting discord was becoming a larger and larger issue for a few members of our congregation. One of our elders, along with someone I thought was my best friend, were leading the charge. We now know they were judging our parenting very harshly. But we did not know it then. We began to sense that something was amiss but we didn't know what was wrong. We knew something was festering, but we didn't know why.

They could have come to us, sat us down, and said "We love you guys. Let's talk about this. We know how wounded Mike is from his childhood. What can we do to help?" Jesus is very concerned about this issue in his Church. He wants the way we treat each other to make a clear statement to a watching world that we Christians love one another. We love one another because of how much Jesus loves us. He gave us a very clear process for addressing sin in Matthew chapter 18. "If your brother or sister sins, go and point out their fault, just between the two of you. If they listen to you, you will have won them over. But if they will not listen, take one or two others along, so that every matter may be established by the testimony of two or three witnesses. If they still refuse to listen, tell it to the church."

But our church elders did not do this. Instead, they did what we Christians do so well.

Gossip and chatter. They started talking among themselves. It's not that their concerns were not valid. They certainly were! And this could have been an opportunity to embody God to Mike - to bring him the healing and comfort that God so desired for him. This was a prime opportunity to *be the church* as Jesus intended the church to be. After all, isn't the mission of the church to bring Jesus to broken, hurting, despairing, sinful men and women? Isn't the mission of the church to demonstrate that God is enough for every corner of our hearts, no matter how dark?

Instead of that, the freight train of gossip and judgment started cutting a swath of destruction through our congregation. Dear friends became enemies. Trust was replaced by suspicion. The fragile, loving community that was such a strong demonstration of the grace and beauty that Jesus can create among people became a huge nasty mess.

In the midst of this, and while we were still pretty clueless as to what was going on, we decided to sell our beloved little pink house. I had a client who was a realtor. May I blame this all on her? She absolutely loved our house, and convinced us that we had enough equity in it to sell it for enough to buy a less imposing home free and clear. That meant no mortgage payment. That meant that I would be able to stop work and concentrate full time on my boys. Mike and I both wanted me to be home and available to them and their friends.

So we put our house on the market. But months went by without any offers, and it became clear that our realtor had grossly overestimated our home's value. We were forced to look further and further out of the metropolitan area to find home prices that would accomplish our goal. I'm not sure now why we didn't just stop the whole process and stay put. Maybe I had become too emotionally invested in being a stay at home mom.

In hindsight, we would have not made this move. It turned out to be an absolutely wretched decision. It was one of those decisions where you look back and can only wonder what the heck you were thinking. But, after ten months our house sold, and we found an affordable home a ferry ride across Puget Sound. We wouldn't own it free and clear, but we would have a drastically smaller house payment. It would mean a long commute for Mike, but we didn't think that would be a big deal.

We were wrong. Our decision to move proved to be just the excuse the church elders needed to get rid of Mike. In April of 1993, after thirteen years pastoring our church, he got fired.

We did not know until almost two decades later that judgment of our parenting was a huge issue. There may have been other issues, too, but no cause of his dismissal - other than our move - was ever given. By anyone. It may be hard to believe, but we honestly did not have a clue what had happened. We were completely baffled. We knew that there had not been any moral lapse on Mike's part. He wasn't having sex with his secretary. Actually, there was no secretary to be tempted by. He wasn't preaching heresy, or getting cultish, or moving into unorthodoxy. He wasn't even accused of any of those things.

People say that Christians are the only ones who shoot their wounded. That's what it seemed like. People we considered our best friends were all of a sudden acting like enemies. Mike was absolutely devastated. All the abandonment issues from his Dad's desertion of him and his mom came rushing back. All the fears of being unloved and unlovable came back to smother him. Jedd and Tyler were affected equally negatively. All of a sudden these favorite relationships were gone. Not only that, but these same people they loved were attacking their dad. And they dearly loved their dad. So they got really angry at these people, and at God.

Our sins and failures, particularly as parents, coupled with the sin of judgment, had cost Mike not only his job, but his calling in life.

I've used the term "judgment" several times up to this point, but I realize it needs some explanation since the Biblical meaning is often misunderstood. The kind of judgment I'm talking about is not, for instance, when I come to a conclusion about someone's sinful behavior based on the facts. If my son steals something, it's not judgmental to conclude "That was wrong." God Himself has already judged that behavior as wrong when He said "Thou shalt not steal." I am simply agreeing with His judgment. But for me to go on and say "You did this because you are selfish, or thoughtless, or rebellious, or proud, and you are a worthless brat" .... That constitutes the kind of judgment the Bible forbids.

The kind of judgment I'm talking about is when one person reaches a *condemning* conclusion about another person. Judgment is when we humans usurp God's place as the only rightful judge. God is the only one who knows enough to judge us. He is the only one who can see inside us and see what is really going on. The apostle Paul confronts this tendency we have to usurp God in the book of Romans where he asks "Who are you to judge the servant of another?" In other words, he is saying this person is God's servant, not yours, so who do you think you are reaching a conclusion about his worth!

Judgment is reaching a condemning conclusion that says I have the right to decide whether this is a redeemable person. Judgment says I have the ability to discern what he is thinking in his heart, or what motivates him. Judgment thinks things like "I am better than him because...." or "I would never do anything like that." There is no love in judgment, and judgment absolutely destroys relationships. Maybe that is why God expressly forbids this kind of judgment. The Bible is explicit on this. Jesus says in Matthew 7:1 "Do not judge, or you too will be judged."

I was not spared from blame either. A dear friend who wasn't bothered by our parenting sent me a three page letter - diatribe is more accurate - that said the whole thing was my fault because I was so damnably arrogant. Remember that I still did not have a clue what had caused the church to blow apart. This was the first indication I had been given of a reason. So I took this accusation very seriously. I wanted, uncharacteristically, to pay attention to it. I needed to know to what extent I was the cause of my husband's destruction.

I sat in my family room, conflicted and upset, and opened my Bible. God took me to the book of Ephesians. I started reading about all the blessings that God has blessed his children - like me - with. Paul, who wrote this letter to the church in Ephesus, enumerates the blessings we have that God heaps upon us. He reminded me that I was chosen to belong to God before the earth was created, to be His child because of what Jesus did for me. Through Jesus, God gifted me with redemption and the forgiveness of my sins. And He let me know his plan for universe, and for my life beyond death. Wow! Can you see how this makes me want to jump up and down and shout "Hallelujah!" He also promised to work out everything in my life to conform to his plans for me. Paul goes on in Ephesians to make clear that this is not a cause for arrogance. He says

" ...and this not from yourselves, it is the gift of God - not by works, so that no one can boast." (2:8b-9)

It was as if God reached down, grabbed me in a

big hug, and held on tight.

There is a fine line between confidence and arrogance. Webster's Dictionary defines arrogance as "proudly contemptuous. Feeling or showing self importance and contempt or disregard for others." Confidence he defines as "belief in one's own abilities, or belief in somebody to act in a proper, trustworthy, or reliable manner." I was confident, but it was not because of anything I had done. God created me that way. Then He gave me parents, and experiences that for the most part increased and enhanced my confidence. I knew God, and knew how He loved me. My confidence was based on knowing that God was trustworthy and reliable. Knowing that he made promises and kept them. Knowing that He was enough.

Did I ever cross the line from confidence to arrogance? Without a doubt. And whenever I did that, I was forgetting where and Who my confidence came from. Whenever I moved into arrogance, I was replacing God confidence with self importance. Certainly there were times when

I needed correction. I needed to learn how to not stomp on other people. I was beginning to get how unintentionally damaging I could be to those around me. I was in my mid forties, and was just beginning to grasp the impact of my personality type on others less confident than me. I was beginning to understand that I was not universally loved and adored; that everyone did not necessarily love me the way that I loved myself. Since I was normally not hurt or bothered by things other people said or did, I was dismally unaware of how I might be hurting them. I began to realize that when my Dad had referred to me as a "bull in a china shop," he may have been thinking of more than my tendency toward clumsiness. Mike had tried to explain to me that I was about "as sensitive as a train wreck." It was difficult for me to empathize with other people's - even my own husband's - neediness; to weep with those that weep. As you have seen, my instant response was "get over it!" You can see why people thought me arrogant. God had to, and was starting to address this issue in my life. But I knew and believed that I was a loved and privileged child of God.   I knew that was where my confidence was based. So I was able to receive the accusation that it was all my fault, process it in light of God's truth, and not be devastated by it.

My fault or not, our lives had been inalterably affected. Because of our own sins, combined with gossip and the self righteousness and judgment of friends, Mike's mission and calling in life - to pastor, teach, and disciple - had been turned on its ear.   It was akin to General Sherman's march to the sea in the Civil War. Our life would be left like Atlanta after Sherman was done, "smoldering and in ruins, the black smoke rising high in the air, and hanging like a pall over the ruined city."

Was I as judgmental as the people who had judged me and my husband? Probably. Was I angry at the people who we had considered our closest friends? Absolutely. Was I bitter? You bet. Was I going to cling to God and find Him enough to get us through this?   That would remain to be seen.

10 SCRAMBLING TO SURVIVE

Nevertheless, in the midst of all the turmoil and confusion, and without the benefit of hindsight, we did sell the house and move. The first month in our new home it did nothing but rain. This was not a soft, indecisive, maybe-it-will-or-maybe-it-won't, Seattle rain. This was a hard, pounding, angry, debilitating downpour. I remember lying in bed, wide awake in the darkness, listening to the rain thunder on the roof, and rush through the down spouts. It sounded as if the deluge would tear them from the house. "My God," I thought, "what have we done."

Regardless, we had to get on with it. We had mouths to feed, bills to pay, a life to rebuild. The home we bought was a cookie cutter style spec house on one and a half acres of land. We hadn't sold our house for enough to be mortgage free, but we had a much lower house payment. This was helpful since Mike no longer had a job. On the bright side, we thought living in the country would make it easier to continue lowering our cost of living and perhaps become more self sufficient. We could grow vegetables, and raise chickens, and have real chores for our sons to do. Maybe it would help keep them out of trouble! I visualized a trellis dripping with wisteria softening the front of the house. I saw gravel paths edged with perennials wending their way back to the chicken coop where we would house our chickens.

Mike was busy designing this coop in his head. It was going to be wonderful, with details like paned windows, a Dutch door, and a peaked roof with a cupola and weathervane. Building it would not only provide a home for our soon-to-be-acquired chickens, it would give Mikey something to pound on. Taking it out on lumber seemed a healthy way for him to vent his grief and anger and frustration at the church process.

And we were probably stalling because Mike did not have a clue what he was going to do.

Other than when he did part-time jobs in high school, all he had ever done was be a pastor. For twenty three years he had served the church. But out of work pastors are not easily re-employed, especially when they are part of small independent churches and not part of a large denomination. I forget exactly why, but pastors are not eligible for unemployment compensation. Mike had been given a few months severance pay, to give us time to figure out what to do.

Our adjustment to life in the country was proving a bit of a challenge. We were learning that a short ferry ride can take you a world away, and this was definitely a different world than Seattle. Our boys referred to it as "this desolate little place", which probably didn't help their adjustment much.

We tried to get acquainted with the neighbors around us, but received a distinctly cold shoulder. We tried delivering fresh eggs as a get acquainted ploy. Very cold shoulder. We tried to strike up conversation at the mailbox. Gruff rebuff. We slowly realized that these country dwellers were in no way pleased to have land around them turned into more housing, no matter how good looking, can you blame them! And unless you were someone's aunt's second cousin, don't expect a warm welcome.

Fortunately there was a happy exception we were really thankful for. A sweet older couple down the road treated us like family and were our life line.

Every community has its dark side, and this one was no exception. To our total astonishment and chagrin, racism was alive and well. We had raised our boys to be color blind. There was no particular merit in this, it was just a way of life for us. Living in a forward thinking suburb of Seattle, everyone we knew was equally color blind. Jedd and Tyler had cultivated friends of every size, color, religion, and race. So when they started their new school in their new home, that was their modus operandi. This proved to not be a way to win friends and influence these people. Once Jedd started driving, he was pulled over by one of the local deputies almost every time he had a friend of a different color with him in the car.

One of his teachers told us he needed to stop "hanging out with scum." We called the Principal on that one, but to no avail.

Our sons were in very difficult years, they were very rebellious, and their experience in this new milieu was doing nothing to ease their path. We asked Tyler not too long ago how he would encapsulate our experience. Without a moment's thought, and with a trace of both bitterness and humor he said "to hell and back."

Three months after our move we discovered yet another dark side of country life. Septic systems. Now there's a concept. To begin with, the whole idea of a septic system is an arcane, mysterious, and highly suspect notion. Rendering human waste (I don't know how to put it more delicately) innocuous by sending it to a tank in one's back yard seems folly to me. But our system was not a simple tank. Apparently to qualify for an old fashioned simple low tech tank you had to have land that "perked". Perk-ability was determined by digging some holes in your land, filling them with water, and then timing how long it took the holes to drain. Our holes had not only taken too long to drain, they hadn't drained at all. Thus we had a very high tech - read very expensive - above ground system. It was a complex mound of interwoven pipes and ditches and access ports occupying a small foothill in our front yard. It had alarms and bells and whistles. It required roughly the same level of education to maintain as your average atomic bomb. And it took it exactly three months to fail. Fail? Yes, fail. What happens when a very expensive, very complex, very "present in the front yard" septic system fails? You flush the toilet in the house, and in an extraordinarily few minutes that very same assortment of fluids and waste is an odious gurgling little geyser on your front lawn. Nothing like it was ever present in our vision of our wisteria draped country home.

Thankfully we had a year long new home warranty. The call to our contractor shattered the calm. He was no longer in business. He had....fled the scene? No. Gone south for the winter? No. Absconded with all company funds?

No. He had escaped all reach of legal recourse. He had freaking died! The bastard! Our conviction that this move had been an altogether bad idea was deepening.

A failed septic system is, however, a problem readily solved. It just takes money. Lots and lots of money. Soon we had a new high tech septic system, and a new higher house payment. Still no job, and the nice low house payment was gone too.

Time was running out, and no job was to be found, so we decided to test the entrepreneurial waters.

Now, my husband is a modern marvel in many ways. He cooks, without a recipe. He cleans, without being asked. He delivers a fabulous latte, complete with mounds of foam, to me in bed every morning. But, he makes a fairly wretched entrepreneur. This is not his fault, it just doesn't fit his skill set. This did not deter us. It wasn't like we had that many options. We assumed that anyone who could envision, design, and build an absolutely topnotch chicken coop could probably also envision, design, and build topnotch furniture. Country style of course. Our entrepreneurial venture was born.

Michael designed and built, and painted and finished furniture like our lives depended on it, which they did. I worked in the office. "What about being a full time mom?" you say. The part of our plan about me being home to concentrate on being a mom to Jedd and Tyler was definitely not working out. Instead, I was the fulltime-and-then-some office manager. I set up appointments with prospective stores, developed a catalog, and handled the mounds of small business paperwork. Mike and I both worked endless days and long weekends. But honestly, Mike's designs were things of beauty. Spice cabinets that made you want to cook. Beds and dressers and coffee tables and Welsh cupboards that warmed the cockles of your heart. Pieces with names like Emma's bed, Kate's Kupboard, Caspar's Bench, and Hannah's Highboy. Whimsical, sturdy, nostalgic, painted and distressed pieces that cost us much more to build and ship than we could sell them for. We planned to make it up in volume. (Math is not our strong point.)

11 THE DEATH OF OUR BUSINESS

We were working so hard to keep our heads above water that there was no energy to think about what was happening, or what it all meant. We had no idea what God was up to. Hadn't we given our lives to serving Him, and leading others to Him? And look where it had gotten us. The main joy in our life came from the damn chickens. I was no longer feeling like God was enough. I was more like numb.

Six years went by. We actually stuck it out for six years. We traveled to trade shows and hawked our goods. And stores actually bought them! A couple of national magazines featured some of our pieces, and sales soared. We had two employees to help us with the sanding, painting, and finishing. And our sons were heavily involved. Tyler was the distressing department. Jedd was our shipping supervisor. Did you know that if you are a small insignificant company, you have to pay the trucking companies for goods they "deliver", before they will consider any claim for damage? What a wonderful scam! I picked up the phone in our office one morning. It was one of our customers on the East Coast. "The truck just arrived with our shipment" she said. "Yeah!" I said. "Not really" she replied. "The driver delivered it by pushing our furniture pieces to the edge of the truck bed, and then letting them crash to the concrete below". Lovely. Lots of smashed furniture, and a shipping company that says "it never happened". We had to rebuild, paint, and finish each piece of furniture that store ordered, and pay to ship it again. Small wonder this was not working out very well financially.

But we kept borrowing capital to keep the business going, and used credit to keep our personal needs met. We were hoping beyond hope that we would turn a profit soon, and then be so successful that we could sell the business for millions, and Mikey could go back to preaching. Don't laugh, that was really my goal. "Five years, five million" was my plan. We would have enough money that he could go back to preaching, but this time his family's financial welfare would not be at the mercy of a congregation. It turned out to be a pipe dream. Mike's designs started showing up in the catalogs of other furniture companies. It turns out that there is really no way to patent a furniture design. The smallest little tweak in the design by the competing company makes their absconding with the design A-OK. Plus, these companies were old and established, and seemed to have a much better grip on building furniture for a profit than we did. It was the beginning of the end.

The boys were done with high school and were making their own way. Despite all our efforts, the ten hour days, and the working weekends, our furniture business was not making us any money. It was, in fact, driving us deeply into debt. I was not happy with God. We talked to Him, and sought his help and guidance, but I gave up expecting that he would do anything. After all, I reasoned, there were Christians all over the world who were struggling to survive just like we were, or worse yet, who were starving, or being persecuted and killed.

There were moments when I wondered where my God was. Where was the God who brought us miracle babies, who reached down and saved Jedd's life; the God who so tenderly and firmly surrounded me when I lived in Japan; the God who brought Francis Schaeffer from Switzerland to my school. Where was he now? I couldn't even approach the question I had spent so much of my life addressing. Was God enough? How could I answer that question when all of life was consumed with just trying to survive.

Finally we kissed the chickens goodbye and moved back to the city. And I got a job. My interior design resume made it much easier for me to get a real job than for Mike to. So I went to work as an interior designer in a retail furniture store, and for a time Mike became the chief cook and bottle washer. I did not know how to sort the experience of the last few years. I knew that God was involved in it somehow, but I could not see how it had been anything but disastrous.

12 STILL SCRAMBLING

My parents always claimed I was able to sell refrigerators to Eskimos. It was clear to them that I was a born salesman. That ability, added to my love of designing homes and rooms for people, made me very successful in my new job. I was making more money than we ever had. Of course, I needed to because we had shut down the business, but had refused to go bankrupt. We did not want to leave our business partner, or our suppliers, holding the bag, so we took on a ton of debt. Well over six figures of debt. I was earning a lot of money, but it took most of what I was making to pay the bills and service the debt.

But we were happy. Mike was having a wonderful time at home. He woke me in the morning with a latte, and I came home at night to a waiting glass of wine and a fabulous dinner. He loved to take care of me, and to take care of the little condo we had purchased. It was only 800 square feet. It was like living on a boat, and we loved it. It forced us to live with just the essentials. My mom never threw anything away. She even kept 40 years worth of rubber bands. As a result, I threw everything away, whether we needed it or not. So I loved this "like we were on a ship" style of living. We wonder now, with grim humor, if God was preparing us for living in our car.

Mike cooked like a pro, and dinners were wonderful. He made things like calamari in piccata sauce, or chicken in white wine reduction with brown rice, or crustade de coq au vin, or pasta with sautéed leeks. We were making new friends at my store, and we loved to have them over for dinner. We have always loved hospitality, and setting a beautiful table, and serving our company. We love to make people feel like they are special, like they are worth going to a great deal of trouble for, to demonstrate as best we can something of the love and creativity of God.

But at the same time, we were having difficulty figuring out how God's love and creativity were at work in our own lives, given what we'd been through. We just could not make sense of it. It remained an unanswered question as we plodded on, and I see now that I grew distant and cool in my relationship with Him. And my job in retail gave me the perfect excuse to skip church on Sunday mornings. After all, I had to be in my store by eleven AM.

But we would occasionally talk about how life would have been different if we had never moved to the country, and if I had gone to work in retail as soon as Michael lost his job, instead of us working together in our furniture business. We would have made plenty of money, and we would not have had a ton of debt. This was definitely an unproductive and anger producing conversation. We discussed the motivation for our move. Had it been based in fear? Had we been concentrating on the "what ifs" in life instead of on who our God was? Had the whole thing been an attempt to secure a less tenuous future? And was that bad, anyway? Was God determined to keep us broke?

Was it only when we were broke that we seriously turned to him?

It must be said that I knew our circumstances were not all God's fault. It would be completely wrong on my part to lay the blame at His feet. Mike and I were hardly the king and queen of financial wisdom. But God's plan for us did not seem to include prosperity. Take our experience with investing. When our church was in its infancy, the elders wanted to make sure that they were helping to provide for Mike's retirement. So they gave us $2000, a very generous sum in 1980, to invest in a retirement account. If I remember correctly, they also gave us the name of the financial advisor we went to see. We made an appointment with him. He was a funny little man. He had permed his hair into absurdly tight little curls. He reminded us of a cross between Chucko the Clown, and Danny Kaye. That alone should have given us cause to reflect, but it didn't. He recommended that we put our money into Public Storage. There were lots of other options out there. Microsoft, for instance. Microsoft was just starting up in our neighborhood, and Mike asked if that might not be a good investment. Our advisor insisted that Public Storage was our best option. We probably should have gotten a second opinion, but instead, we handed him our money. For reasons that are way beyond my grasp, our investment was in a retirement instrument that did not allow us access it in any way for twenty years. Our advisor insisted that we could not roll it over into a different instrument, even if we paid a penalty. We were stuck. In 2001, when the money was finally accessible to us again, the $2000 had grown to $2600. Unfortunately I am not joking. We could have done better in a standard savings account! We could have done much better in the stock market. And if we had invested in Microsoft? A well meaning but rather gleeful friend sat down and figured out how much our $2000 would have grown to if we had let it sit untouched for twenty years through all Microsoft's growth, and through all the stock splits. He figured our $2000 would have grown to something over four million dollars. How does one sort this?! It wasn't even our fault, it was just bad advice.

What I did know was that working on straight commission was starting to stress me out. I never knew from one month to the next what our income would be, and although I continued to do well, their was an inner turmoil that was making me tired and angry. Israel's ancient King David nailed what I was feeling in Psalm 30: 6-9.

"When I was prosperous I said 'Nothing can stop me now!' Your favor made me as secure as a mountain. Then you turned away from me and I was shattered. I cried out to you, O Lord. I begged the Lord for mercy, saying 'What will you gain if I die, if I sink into the grave? Can my dust praise you? Can it tell of your faithfulness?'"

I didn't know what God was up to, but I know now that there was an anger toward Him starting to build in me that I was not yet in touch with.

13 THE DEATH OF PASTORING

Perhaps you are wondering why Mike didn't go back to being a pastor? Ah ha. That is what my dad would call a loaded question.

When Mike was a young man just starting to pursue his calling as a pastor, a very wise man told him that unless you absolutely had to be a pastor, avoid it like the plague. Pastors are targets for people's judgments, are blamed for their frustrated expectations, and are not allowed the failings of every day Christians. And that is just for starters. If you don't believe in invisible, evil, destructive powers at war with God and His people, just try being a pastor. You will believe in a hurry.

The pastor of our new church relates a telling story. For some reason he was visiting another church. Good Presbyterian that he is, he was sitting in the very back pew. He was feeling particularly weary and battered. The service included a dramatic presentation of the life of Moses, when God was calling Moses to pastor the people of Israel. While Moses was considering how to answer, our pastor found himself thinking "say no, say no!" As soon as he thought that, he heard someone call his name. He heard it so clearly that he turned around to see who it was. But there was no one there. Then he heard God say to him, "I know you feel used up, but I still want to use you." Our pastor found himself bawling in the pew. The man who was sitting closest to him immediately moved as far away from him as it was possible to get. That is what it can be like to be a pastor.

To weather such a calling, you have to have a fire in your belly that will not allow you to do anything else. For twenty three years Mike's belly fire had stayed stoked. But when our church imploded, the fire became more like a burning barn. The kind of burning barn you seriously do not want to go back into. It was such a grief, because he is a fine preacher and mentor. I remember one Easter Sunday when he was preaching at the church we had gone to ever since the death of our church. He lined up five small squishy furry stuffed Easter bunnies in a horizontal line across the platform. He labeled each one with a theory posited for why Jesus' resurrection from the dead cannot be true. Then he carefully and methodically demonstrated from the historical record and eye witness testimony why each theory was indefensible. He emphasized the point by taking a seven iron, and point by point golfing each little bunny into the congregation. The children in the congregation were ecstatic. It was a wonderful and unforgettable visual illustration.

We were talking about this the other day, and Mike said the bottom line was that he lost the boldness required to be a pastor. It takes boldness to proclaim that there is truth to a world that mocks the concept. It takes boldness to enter people's lives, share their most intimate secrets, and believe that God is going to give you something worthwhile for that person. And he didn't feel bold, he felt like a failure. He felt timid, fearful, and insecure. He felt like no church would want him after the way our church ended. After all, it does not look that well on a resume.

The other reason Mike did not go back into ministry was me. I did not make it easy for my husband to return to pastoring. How it pains me to say this! It was not because I didn't want him to. It was because of who I am, or more accurately, who I am perceived to be. Many people have very particular expectations for pastors' wives, and I definitely don't fit the mold. Mike had been doing quite a bit of preaching at the church we were going to. He was mentoring and teaching groups of young men. In a significant way he was doing the work of a pastor. Eventually when it came time for the pastor of our church to retire, there was some talk of hiring Mike to replace him. It was not to be. One of the men who headed the pastoral search committee paid me a visit. His message was clear. Even had Mike been ready to return to ministry, it would never happen, largely because of me. He explained to me in no uncertain terms that I made a lousy pastor's wife. I was an interior designer, for Pete's sake! It certainly doesn't take very many fingers on very many hands to count the number of pastor's wives who are also interior designers. After all, aren't interior designers by nature more concerned with things and stuff than people? My love of interior design had been an issue for Christians around us since the earliest days of Mike's ministry. I had had to study the Bible, and build a theology of interior design in order to communicate to those who asked, how such a profession could be appropriate for a Christian woman, much less a pastor's wife. I saw interior design as a way to build rooms and create spaces that emphasized the importance of caring for people. I designed rooms that welcomed family, friends, and strangers in; that welcomed them to sit down and stay a while; to put their feet up and get comfortable. And I saw interior design as a way to demonstrate God's love of beauty, and color, and creativity. One only has to look at the extravagant, unnecessary, abundant splendor of creation to see that God cares about the environment we live in. But sadly that can be a difficult concept for some Christians.

However, my career was not the only thing that disqualified Mike in this gentleman's opinion. It wasn't even his major problem. Who I am was his major problem. Someone who has become a dear friend told me that when she first met me she thought I was "powerful and terrifying." Ouch! I very much do not see myself that way! I blubber like a baby through The Star Spangled Banner. A gorgeous sunset reduces me to tears. I wept when my son laid his first born son in my arms. He was so stunning, so gorgeous, so beautiful, so perfect, so brown! so tiny. Actually he still is, except for the tiny part. Can you understand why I struggle? I see myself as a fuzz ball! OK, maybe a powerful and terrifying fuzz ball, but a fuzz ball nonetheless.

Here's the problem. Jesus' church has the unique privilege of being the vessel containing the gracious, liberating, affirming, healing love of God.

Its task is to pour that love out on each other with the same kindness and generosity that Jesus demonstrated when he lived among us. And yet we often squander that privilege through our judgments, narrowing people's lives rather than widening them. Sometimes we have such a narrow view of what a Christian should look like that we stuff people into an arbitrary mold of emaciated spirituality. It becomes a straight jacket that squeezes the life out of us. Its like we take God's creation, with all its color and variety and texture and beauty, and try to turn it to black and white. The result is that many of us are filled with guilty and hopeless feelings because we don't fit into the mold. Others are angry and rebellious because they think God is like we so often are - mean and colorless and annoyed with others' uniqueness. One of my favorite hymns addresses this so well.

> "There's a wideness in God's mercy like the wideness of the sea;
> There's a kindness in His justice which is more than liberty.

But we make His love too narrow by false limits of our own;

And we magnify his strictness with a zeal He will not own."

While religion in its worst form tries to make us all the same, God wants us to soar like eagles, not squawk like parrots. God created each of us uniquely. Only as we are true to the person God made us to be do we really fulfill our special role in His plan for the universe.

Jesus showed us that we experience our purpose and destiny not when we bow to the pressures around us to be like somebody else, not when we try to be religious, but only when we stick to being ourselves. When He lived here on earth, He demonstrated that He is a mold-breaker. He is a liberator. His first miracle was to turn water into wine. His favorite people to hang out with were prostitutes like the woman at the well, and extortionists like Zaccheus, and tough, gruff fishermen like Peter, James, and John - people just like you and me. He loved going to parties, and telling interesting jokes and stories, and eating and drinking and celebrating with all kinds of people as he demonstrated to them the love and goodness of God.   Jesus showed us one aspect of what being a "Christian" looks like.   It is a deep commitment to never compromise our true self, no matter the criticism from the religious establishment, and to offer that same grace and acceptance to those around us.

"Religion" is never enough. It is not enough to make our lives complete, or to give us purpose and meaning.   But a relationship with Jesus is more than enough because He is the one who created me to be me, and who helps me discover how to be me through the trials and pressures of life

The fact that I was born confident made it easier for me than for most, to weather the kind of judgments that have come my way. God gifted me with a confidence that has always allowed me to say "don't mess with me." But this does not come from a misplaced sense of my own importance. Rather, it comes from my relationship with Jesus. It comes out of the confidence I have in the truth that God made me the way I am, loves me the way

I am, and doesn't want me to try to be somebody else. This is an immensely significant aspect of how God is enough for me. The very essence of who I uniquely am is not a cosmic accident, or something to apologize for, or to be ashamed of. I absolutely know that I am intrinsically valuable exactly the way God designed me. I have this confidence because God gave me a dad that modeled that kind of love. I have this confidence because Mike has never made me feel like I should see myself any differently. Far from blaming me for any of the complications around his calling, he has always wanted me to be true to the way God made me irrespective of how other people might react. And I have this confidence because the Bible shows very clearly that this is how Jesus loves me, and how He loves you. Being loved in this way by the God of all creation is no small thing. It is very much at the center of knowing and experiencing that HE IS ENOUGH.

I wish I had had the maturity and grace to dialogue this with the man from the pastoral committee. Looking back, I wish I had poured us both a glass of wine. I wish I had looked him in the eye, and asked him if he really understood, if he really meant, what he was saying. But, in that moment, all I wanted was for him to get out of my house.

So that was that. Mike was not going to be given the opportunity to be a pastor again, at least not in that situation.

Our sons were not wild about their Dad being a pastor again, anyway. Mike remembers with awful clarity the night almost two decades ago when he came home from the meeting that would determine if our church would continue on, or disband. Jedd and Tyler and I were sitting in our family room, waiting for the sound of Mike's car coming up the long gravel driveway. When he finally came through the door, he looked at me and said one word. "Disband." Tyler was stunned. "You mean, Daddy," he said with tears running down his face, "that our church doesn't exist anymore?" It broke Tyler's heart, and it broke something else in him as well. Over time, he decided that Christians were hypocrites, and that the church was worthy only of his scorn. He decided that he was going to do whatever he wanted, God and his parents be damned. It was the start of a long dark journey for him, and it was years before we had our Tyler back. Jedd, on the other hand, is a burier and a stuffer. He hid his grief like a hard stone, wrapped in a coating of anger, stuck perpetually in his craw. They would attend church only if their father was preaching, and even then they would come late and leave early. Still today, both of our sons will have very little to do with church. They do each, in their own way, have a relationship with Jesus, and they each teach their children about Jesus, in their own way. Still both of them are very cynical toward, and quick to judge other Christians. But we are so thankful that they have a great relationship with us. They love us, seek us out, communicate with us, play with us, text us. We could not ask more from our sons in terms of how they relate to us. I've even achieved top-ten friend status on Tyler's Facebook. In terms of their walk with God, we pray, and dialogue, and listen and encourage. But in the end - I heard it put so well recently - children of believing parents must find their way to God on their own legs and their own feet.

You may be wondering if it wasn't about time that we just got over the church thing! We felt the same way! Why wouldn't the acute, stifling, overwhelming pain that we felt when our church rejected Mike finally recede and go away!? I was the queen of expecting people to get over stuff, but we couldn't get over this. Mikey and I would look at each other. "Come on!" we would say. "Its been three, (then five, then ten, then fifteen) years! Its time to move on, buck up, grow up." But we couldn't seem to. It was a mountain whose summit we could not seem to scale.

14 GRANDBABIES

In the meantime our family was burgeoning. Both boys had married and were producing children. Jedd and his wife gifted us with a beautiful baby grandson. Tyler and his wife produced a gorgeous baby girl a year and a half later. I wasn't sure my heart could handle being a grandma. I thought it might burst with the love I felt for those children, and the joy they brought me. A picture I sent to my siblings said it all. I am holding BooBoo, who is Jedd's oldest. He's about eight months old. He is wearing a little red baseball cap. We are nose to nose, and he is cupping my face with his pudgy little hands. Mutual adoration oozes from the picture. Caption? "I'm adjusting pretty well to this grandma thing." Who can dispute that grandchildren are really a vast improvement on children! You can have them when and where you want them, and send them home when you are done. You can spoil them rotten without the slightest guilt, and then give them back to their parents. It's the ultimate payback.

All five of our grandchildren arrived within three and a half years of each other, and three of them within two months. Grandbabies number three and four were twin girls born to Jedd and Teri, and Tyler had our fifth, baby Kai, two months later. When those three were born, BooBoo was three, and Tyler's oldest, Leilani, was eighteen months. It made quite an impact on any family gathering. You can picture it; 3 car seats, 3 diaper changing pads, three "keep the baby occupied" toys, plus a toddler and a three year old. It was quite a crush in our little condo. Even though these children are one of the great delights of my life, I will use them to excuse the next really unfortunate thing Mike and I did. We decided to buy a bigger house. It is not that there is anything inherently wrong in buying a bigger house. And we didn't even buy a house that was as big as the bank said we could afford. But the economic tsunami of 2007 was about to rush ashore.

15 THE LORD GIVETH AND THE LORD TAKETH AWAY

I was starting to feel the deteriorating economy at work. People were not coming in to buy furniture in nearly the numbers I was used to. My income was on a downward spiral. I was, after all, paid on straight commission. But we weren't too concerned yet. After all, I had been doing really well for several years, and how bad could it get, anyway! Our mortgage banker was not concerned either. Everybody seemed to think this was an economic bump that we would climb over in no time, and things would go back to normal.

Mike and our realtor, not the one from Kirkland but a dear friend of many years, went searching for a house for us. They called me at work one day, and said they had found the perfect place. It was in a "55 and older" community. That concept alone should have made us think twice. It was hard to think of ourselves as that old, and it made us feel even older since all of our neighbors were 80 plus. The up side was that they were mostly really sweet folks who treated us like "young whipper-snappers." There was one dear old guy across the street who was nearing 80, but was as out of touch with his age as we were with ours. He came hobbling across the street one morning soon after we moved in and told us in a conspiratorial manner that "we younger folks in the neighborhood have to stick together."

Our realtor thought it would be a fabulous investment. All the baby boomers that were retiring in a few years would be looking for places just like this to buy. It was a terribly dated little 1200 square foot rambler, but one walk through, and I could see how moving a wall here, and knocking out a wall there, could give us a great-room and kitchen that would be fabulous for hospitality, as well as giving our family ample room to eat and play. Mike was in love with the idea of what we could make this house become, so we bought it, and then invested most of our savings in remodeling it. My dad had always said that real estate was never a bad investment. Certainly more reliable than the stock market, he had always said. And our realtor said that new retirees would be falling all over us to buy a fully remodeled house in this community. So we forged ahead.

To make this fairly extensive remodel affordable Mike and our realtor friend did all the work. I watched with glee as walls came down and spaces opened up. Hallways were widened and kitchen and living room became one great-room. Jedd, Tyler, Mike, and even BooBoo ripped up ugly old carpets and replaced them with gleaming wood floors. I came home from work the night the floors were finished, peeked through the front porch window, and reveled in the soft warm glow of oak flooring that stretched from the front door, past the kitchen, and into the back bedrooms. This was a floor that would stand up to the constant flow of grandchildren, friends, guests, strangers in need, and the young men Michael was mentoring. Our daughter-in-law Teri, who is Samoan, had put all her aboriginal energy into scraping popcorn off the ceilings. The walls were painted a buttery khaki, and were finished off with beautiful crown moldings and deep baseboards. The ample granite covered kitchen island held Mikey's pride and joy, a 6-burner gas cook top, and my pride and joy, our grandchildren. They often clamored up onto the stools, spoons in hand, and waited eagerly for whatever concoction Grandpa would produce. This house had been such a family endeavor, and our family was planning to enjoy it for many years to come. On the high wall spanning the space between the kitchen and the kitchen nook we stenciled in large chocolate colored letters "We have pitched our tent in the land of hope". But as the poet Robert Burns so aptly said, the best laid plans of mice and men often go awry.

We bought the house at the exact top of the market in Seattle, December of 2007. We signed the papers just about the same day that the market started to crash.

When I said that my favorite hymn was "I'd rather have Jesus than houses or lands", I really didn't think that it would come to that. But three and one half years after buying our little house, we were in foreclosure.

We had lost everything, every cent we had put into it. It had been hard to tell which had tanked faster, my income, or the value of the house. The recession had destroyed everything for a lot of people, and we were among them.

Mike had eventually gone back to work in sales. His love of people and sense of humor made him a great addition to a sales team. But when the economy faltered, he was laid off, and like so many men his age, prospects for finding employment were bleak. Then a few weeks after being laid off, his back finally said "you've abused me long enough" and blew up on him. He had surgery as a last resort, but although that relieved some of his pain, he did not regain his mobility.

We had both turned 60 that year. We were at the age where it would have been nice to contemplate retirement. Instead, our house was being foreclosed on, and we were being forced into bankruptcy. Our sons suggested somewhat wryly that we change the stencil in the kitchen to "the Lord giveth and the Lord taketh away."

You can imagine our chagrin. Hadn't we taken on huge debt a decade earlier to avoid bankruptcy? Hadn't I worked really hard to make enough money to pay the debt so that we wouldn't have to go bankrupt? I felt so incredibly betrayed. Stupid? That too. But there was no avoiding it now.

I kept up a pretty brave front. "It's just a house," I would say. "It's only money," I would say. "It's not like I am losing Michael, or the boys, or the grandbabies.....it's just stuff."

I was in serious denial.

16 RETIREMENT? NOT LIKELY

The foreclosure was proceeding, and we needed to move, but we did not know what to do, where to go next, how to move on. Should we throw the towel in and find a cheap place to retire? An out of the USA place, perhaps?

"How about a tropical paradise?" Teri's parents suggested. They had recently retired and moved back to their island home of Samoa, where they were living very comfortably, thank you, on social security.

If you are hazy about exactly where Samoa is, you are not alone. When I called my brother to tell him we were going to go to Samoa, he sounded quite alarmed. "Aren't there pirates there" he queried? "Not Somalia!" I exclaimed, while trying to hide my hoots of laughter. "Samoa!" "Oh" he said, clearly not convinced. Samoa is a grouping of lovely islands in the South Pacific, somewhere between the equator and New

Zealand. It is a tropical paradise, and that sounded really good to me. I've always been a sun person, a beach person, a person able to happily do absolutely nothing but snooze on a lounge chair. Teri's parents invited our whole family for a visit. It was quite an excursion. Jedd and Teri and the twins and BooBoo, Tyler and his kids, and Mike and I, all took a ten hour plane trip across the Pacific to exotic Polynesia.

I should mention, in case you have noticed that I never talk about Tyler's wife, that she abandoned him and the children when Baby Kai was just over a year old. She married Tyler thinking that he would bring her happiness and fulfillment, but it did not take very many years for her to realize that Tyler was not enough, and not even her beautiful children were enough, to satisfy the deep longings of her heart. So she left her family and embarked on a destructive, still ongoing journey to find someone, something, to fill the void in her heart. Tyler is slowly recovering, and even though he is both alone and lonely, he is a faithful, wonderful, and loving single dad, and his children adore him.

Anyway, this flight across the Pacific was a red eye that left LAX at midnight. We were flying Air New Zealand, which is really an intelligent airline. They wined us and dined us into a stupor, so we all slept like babies the whole way, even the kiddos. We landed in Samoa at five o'clock on a summer morning. Actually it was summer in Seattle, but winter in Samoa. Some winter! It was already 75 degrees, and the humidity wrapped around us like a wet blanket. A steaming hot wet blanket. But the palms trees stood erect and beautiful, the tropical sun was approaching the horizon, and rays of brilliant color were streaking across the sky. It was absolutely stunning.

We spent a fabulous ten days there. Actually, the family and I spent a fabulous ten days. Mikey was miserable the whole time. The only time he wasn't dying of heat prostration was when he was in the ocean. And what an ocean! Turquoise blue, crystal clear, bathtub warm water that lapped onto sparkling white sandy beaches. The grandkids will never again consider a Western

Washington beach a real beach. They splashed and played in the shallows while their parents snorkeled amid the coral reefs that stood just offshore. I could have watched for hours as the great waves pounded against the reefs in a huge spray of sky-flung foam and thunder. It was awesome. I took long walks early every morning, a couple of grandchildren by the hand, the others gamboling around me in the surf, our toes in the water, scouring the beach for the shells that washed ashore every night. On my coffee table now is a collection of sun-bleached giant clam shells. How could anyone look at this shell and not believe in a Creator? Gleaming pearlescent on the inside and perfectly formed ruffled and scalloped ridges on the outside. Beauty for no reason, except God's creative extravagance.

I was in heaven. Unfortunately, Mikey was in hell. It certainly was hot. If you took a taxi ride, by the time you reached your destination, you, your clothes, and the car upholstery were soaked through with perspiration. I smelled like a pole cat most of the time. And even though it was populated by the sweetest, kindest, happiest, most welcoming people, it was a third-world country. Power was allotted on a rolling black-out basis. Ice-cold water for the showers, torturous even in this climate, came out of an un-adorned pipe - yes, a pipe - from the ceiling. You could only get back to the USA once a week, and that assumed your plane did not develop engine trouble - which ours did. We were sitting in our plane on the steaming tarmac, ready to go home. The safety tape started playing but the plane did not start its usual roll-back from the gate. The tape finished and the plane still sat stubbornly motionless. Mike and I gave each other a long, worried look. After a few minutes the loud-speaker crackled to life; "This is your captain speaking. We have had catastrophic engine failure, and this plane will not be leaving Samoa tonight." What happens when you have engine failure on the only plane leaving a small, remote island in the middle of the South Pacific that week? You wait for mechanics and parts to arrive from New Zealand, and it's another day in paradise, or hell, depending on your perspective.

I can assure you that we were very thankful the engine trouble occurred while we were still on the ground rather than over the Pacific ocean. But that was the straw that broke this particular camel's back. Samoa was too hot, too primitive, and too remote. So what was plan B? I would keep working, but in California.

Renting an apartment when you have a bankruptcy and foreclosure on your credit report can be problematic at best. But we found that it seemed to be less problematic in California than in Washington. Mike was a California boy at heart, and I was beyond sick of rain and gray. Samoa had given me a taste of living in sunshine. Mike is convinced that I have at least some degree of Seasonal Affective Disorder. And since he has to put up with me on a daily basis, he should know. All I know is, when I wake up in the morning to the sun pouring in the window, I jump out of bed eager to face whatever the day will bring. I love to turn my face to the sun and just bask in its warmth and joy. But when I wake up to gray cloud cover, or rain, I want to dive back under the covers and stay there. Pouting. Even the proximity to our family could not overcome my antipathy to Seattle's weather. It is a testament to my husband's deep love for me that he did nothing to discourage us from making this move. Even though it meant leaving behind life-long friends; leaving the relationships that were so important to us; leaving the church that had been our home for years, and where Mikey felt loved and safe; even though it meant leaving behind the ministry to young men that was so important to him; even though it meant pulling up roots that went deep and wide, Mike did not discourage me from moving to a place where we did not know a soul.

So, we sold or gave the kids most of the furniture we had left, keeping just enough to furnish a one bedroom apartment, and moved to California.

You know, I put that in black and white, and think, wow, wasn't moving to a new state and a new job awfully risky, even stupid? After all, we were almost 61 years old! Well, the bottom line is that we had already lost just about everything, and Seattle's weather had gotten to me that much. Plus, even in this economic downturn, and even at my age, my resume meant I was able to get a job pretty easily. We chose to move to the Sonoma County wine country just north of San Francisco, to the lovely little city of Santa Rosa. The internet assured me there were only 70 days of rain a year on average in Santa Rosa, as compared to Seattle's 250 days. It meant leaving Jedd and Teri, and Tyler and the grandchildren behind, but they could visit us often. It was, after all, a pretty quick trip straight down Interstate Five. And we were able to lease a great little apartment without too much hassle.

So now we are back where this story started in August 2010. We packed up everything we owned, got into our 2006 Scion XB, which was the only car the bankruptcy had left us, and with one last look back at our little house, followed the U-Haul truck driven by Jedd with BooBoo buckled in next to him, down Interstate Five toward California.

Our first day in Santa Rosa the temperature

was 106. It was the hottest day in that city in 79 years. It was bright, crystal clear, and the heat was dry and velvety. BooBoo, Jedd, and I went to the pool to swim and bask in the sun. Mikey basked in our apartment, which thankfully for him is air conditioned. The next day we put our son and grandson on a plane back to Seattle, and there we were, alone in our new home.

We could see God's hand in the location of our apartment. We had picked the complex when I was in Santa Rosa interviewing, but had not seen the actual apartment that we leased. It turned out to be in the loveliest possible part of the complex, a corner unit, with a welcoming shaded patio, across from a green belt and Santa Rosa creek. We looked at the other units, some baking in the afternoon sun, some fronting the highway, and were so thankful for the apartment we had been given.

And I was loving our part of California and its weather. I would stand out in the sun with my head thrown back and arms thrown wide drinking it in. Fall was filled with sunny warm days, with deep sapphire blue skies, and sparkling light. On my days off we went on long drives, through acre after acre of vineyards, passing vines heavy with grapes. I still marvel over the texture of the landscape - the verdant vines, the gnarly oak trees, the majestic redwoods, and the nut brown hills. It is a magical mix. The air is full of the most enticing scents; that only California blend of arid eucalyptus, jasmine, herbs, and wine. And dead skunk. I don't know what it is about skunks here, but they have no ability to get from one side of the road to the other in one piece!

Mike and I had often talked about how great it would be to live some place where we could actually grow citrus, so our first purchase for our new home was a small Meyer lemon tree, and it is flourishing on our patio, covered with luscious yellow fruit. We found an organic farmers' produce stand, and an organic strawberry farm close to home, and we were eating yummy ripe strawberries into November. Jedd and Teri and the kids came to visit us in October, and we stopped with them at the strawberry farm and bought a half flat of berries. The children started eating them in the car and had demolished the entire flat by bedtime. The next morning the twins, Alyssa and Alexis, came out of the bedroom and crawled into my arms. "Grandma", they whispered, "more strawberries?"

On one of our exploring drives we came across an organic heirloom tomato stand. It was piled high with orange, red, yellow, and purple, warm, freshly picked, ripe tomatoes. The sign that gave the prices also said to leave payment in the supplied box. The honor system! Amazing. We made our choices and paid our money. Mike stopped at a shop that had been recommended to us for a freshly risen, ready to cook pizza dough. At home, he covered the dough with olive oil, roasted pine nuts, garlic, and thin slices of heirloom tomatoes. As it baked the aroma filled our apartment, and eating it was like eating candy.

The first week of November, which was cold and rainy in Seattle, was 84 degrees and sunny in Santa Rosa. On Thanksgiving Day our children and grandchildren were snowed in in Seattle. In contrast, we took the 40 minute drive to the ocean, and had a glass of wine in the sparkling sunshine on the patio of a small restaurant overlooking the water. The weather part of this move was working out really well. And Mike and I were having such a good time together. It had been over thirty years since it had been just the two of us, and it was wonderful to once again revel in each other's company.

But we needed to find a church, and make some new friends. And I was going to learn that God had not given up on me. I had distanced myself from Him, but He had never let go of my hand.

17 GOD SPEAKS

Our search for a new church resulted in our attending a small group meeting one Saturday night. I don't remember what we were supposed to be discussing, but one of the women in the group starting telling us about her experience with God. She came from a wealthy family, she said, and she had found that God always provided his children's needs. I sat in my chair, rigid, still as a stone. If I moved I knew I would rise to my feet and scream at the top of my lungs, "HE DOES NOT! HE MOST CERTAINLY DOES NOT!" As I sat there, immobilized, it was like someone split me open from stem to stern, and I saw all this anger; this visceral, boiling, popping-vein-in-the-forehead anger at God that filled me like black inky venom.

I held myself together until the meeting finally ended, although I'm sure the people there thought I was the single most unfriendly person they had ever met. Once home, I collapsed into tears. Poor

Mikey. "What's the matter, sweetheart?" he asked. I told him about my reaction to the evening, and how it had resulted in an epiphany. I realized that all the "it's just a house" stuff, and all the "it's only money" stuff was covering a black hole of anger in my heart. All the rationalizing I had done about what God was up to when our church fell apart, and when we spent the next six years working our fingers to the bone, for *nothing*, simply masked a simmering fury. And when I finally started earning a good income, but had to throw away a huge amount of that income to pay off the company debt, a growing seething anger at God started to consume me. It was an anger that proved that I had forgotten what I had once been so sure of. The reality that God is enough had dissipated in the years of struggle, and had finally drowned in that frigid cold river of financial ruin.

These words from an old hymn describe so succinctly where I was at this point.
"Souls of men! Why will ye scatter
like a crowd of frightened sheep?
Foolish hearts! Why will you wander

from a love so true and deep?
There's no place where earth's sorrows
are more felt than up in Heaven.
There is no place where earth's failings
have such kindly judgment given."

God was going to use my vitriolic, hysterical, vehement response that Saturday evening to begin a process that I am still in. As you have seen, there had been several pivotal and transformational episodes in my life to this point. The first was when Francis Schaeffer visited my high school. The second was my time in Japan. The third was when I hung those window treatments in our first home. And the fourth was when the death of our church dropped an atomic bomb into our lives. And God, in his "kindly judgment" was not done with me yet.

I was about to enter what in today's vernacular can best be described as the mother of all pivotal moments.

18 IDOLS

This pivotal moment, this chapter in my life, would reveal to me the gravity, the foolishness, the wickedness of what I had done. It would reveal to me how I had forgotten the crucial lessons I had learned as a young woman. It would reveal to me how I had turned my back on the living God, the God whose faithfulness to me had known no measure. It would reveal to me how in a significant way I had completely forgotten what God had impressed on me during those long, lonely nights in Japan so many years ago. Remember how I studied the book of Hosea? Remember how God's people had turned from Him, and had embraced idols? Idols do not satisfy, idols only bring destruction. And they are so insidious. They find a way to creep into our hearts, and once there, they are harder to displace than bed bugs. Remember, I am not talking about little bronze statues in the living room. Those are so obvious, so easy to get rid of.

Into the trash they go, and there! I am idol free. No. I am talking about anything that I value more than I value my relationship with God; anything that I seek more than I seek God; anything that I trust more than I trust God; anything I look to other than God to save me.

In my case, one of my idols was financial security. One of my idols was stress free retirement. One of my idols was freedom from trials and tribulations. And one of my idols was success and well-being for my children and grandchildren.

None of these desires are wrong in themselves. In fact, they are good and right desires. But they became idols when they took God's place in my heart, and when I distanced myself from God because these desires were not being fulfilled.

Over our lattes every morning, Mike and I usually spend some time in the Psalms. Psalm 73 has been the one Psalm that I have lately asked him to read again and again. The title of the Psalm is "God is my strength and my portion." Becky translation - "God is enough." The writer of this Psalm had gone through an experience much like mine. He tells that his feet had almost stumbled, his steps had nearly slipped. He says that his soul was embittered and he was pricked in heart. He had lost sight of God. And then he says something that I could have written.

"I was brutish and ignorant, I was like a beast toward God."

Another translation says "I became senseless before you." This passage from the Bible was like a long, gleaming, razor sharp arrow that went straight from God's bow, thunk, deep into my heart.

Because I had turned to idols, I had become senseless, and numb over the last few years. I had almost totally lost myself, and had become like a beast before God. Some people think that if we give our lives to Jesus, we will lose who we are; our personality will become colorless and uninteresting. The opposite is actually true. Francis Schaeffer addressed this. He said "Some people fear that following Jesus will diminish their personality. What nonsense! Who made the personality!" I know that as I had turned from

God to idols, I had become less than who I could be. I had significantly lost the best of who I was.

I had so not been able to see it. But Mikey had. He had seen my joy dissipate, my heart harden, my blood turn cold. He also knew there was no talking to me about it. I could not hear it. If he were to gingerly approach the subject of my anger and bitterness, the communication door would slam in his face. He says now that I would come in the door from work like a tiger. A fierce, growling tiger, looking for some unfortunate victim to pounce on and devour. The senior pastor at one of Mike's first churches had told him I was an "unusual woman, a woman used of God." Mike and I used to chuckle about that. But I had morphed from that woman into, forgive me - there is no polite way to express this - a complete bitch.

Do you know the story of Job? He was a very rich man, and a man who served and loved God. The Old Testament tells us that Satan came to God one day and asked permission to take all of Job's riches, and even his family, away from him. Satan's assertion was that of course Job loved and served God. Why shouldn't he! God had given him a privileged and insulated life. Satan said to God, "Have you not put a hedge around him and his household and everything he has? But stretch out your hand and strike everything he has, and he will surely curse you to your face." God allowed Satan to destroy Job's wealth, his family, and his health. I know this seems inexplicable. God is often not easy to decipher. C.S. Lewis in his "Chronicles of Narnia" uses the great lion Aslan as a metaphor for Jesus. Lewis makes a statement about what is often our inability to figure out what God is up to. He says, "He is not a tame lion."

God allowed Satan access to Job's life. In a series of devastating events Job's children were all killed, and he lost all his flocks, all his crops, all his money, all his assets. He was left sitting in a heap of ashes, picking at the running sores all over his body, flat broke.

Job did not curse God, but he did accuse Him. He questioned why he was being put through such distress, such pain, such destruction when he had been a righteous man. God spent several chapters of the Bible reminding Job that Job was not God, God was. He asked Job "Where were you?" Where had Job been when God laid the foundations of the earth? Where was Job when the morning stars sang together and all the angels shouted for joy at God's work of creation. "Have you journeyed to the springs of the sea," God asked. "Or walked in the recesses of the deep? What is the way to the abode of light? And where does darkness abide? Can you take them to their places? Do you know the way to their dwellings? Can you raise your voice to the clouds and cover yourself with a flood of water? Do you send the lightening bolts on their way? Do they report to you, 'Here we are?'" After enumerating all of his majestic power and presence in the world, God asked Job "Will he who contends with the Almighty correct Him? Let him who accuses God answer Him!"

I have known this story from my youth, and had always thought that God was basically telling Job to shut up. Or like I would have done, telling him "to get over it." But as I studied it again, I realized that God was actually asking Job my question. He was asking Job if He was enough. In the midst of all the suffering Job was going through, could he see that God alone was enough? God was asking Job if financial security, or his children's welfare, would displace God's place in Job's heart.

I think that God was first trying to help Job see that only He had the power and wisdom and knowledge and competence to create and sustain the entire universe. Then He wanted Job to see, by virtue of the fact that God Himself was there personally explaining this to him, that the apex of God's creation was man himself. Man was created in the very image of God, and as such was meant to exist in fellowship with God, as God's very soul mate, if you will. That's the wonder of it! As far as man is concerned, everything else in the universe, however wonderful, is secondary to this *one* thing - fellowship with God Himself. So when Job lost "everything", he really lost very little compared to the one thing he still had - the love and fellowship of his divine Creator. And so, no matter how terrible and painful Job's experience, the whole point of that experience was to enable him to see the most important thing - that God is enough.

Job's response makes clear that he totally got this. He replied to God, "My ears had heard of you, but now my eyes have seen you. Therefore I despise myself and repent in sack cloth and ashes." He had seen God, so he could say "Though God slay me, yet will I hope in Him." From his ash heap, from his seemingly hopeless situation, Job asserted that God was enough.

I mulled on this story. Perhaps like Job, God had allowed the destructive events of my life to test my commitment to Him. First He had given me a firm and stable foundation to anchor to. He had brought Francis Schaeffer into my life to teach me that He was enough to answer all my basic philosophical questions. Then He took me to Japan to teach me that He was enough even if I remained single and alone my entire life. Then He allowed me to experience the anguish of infertility to show me that He was enough, even if we never had children. He showed me his miraculous power when he gifted me with my precious boys.

Then He let me experience the destructive power of judgment, to show me that He was enough for me to survive the attacks of even my closest friends. So far so good. But then He let the winds and storms of life start to rail against that foundation. He put me through years of financial hardship and struggle, even let us lose our house and our assets, because He wanted me to whole heartedly, enthusiastically, from the roof tops, exclaim the answer to the question "Is God enough?" He wanted me to not falter when our house was gone, our savings were gone, and I faced a bleak non-retirement where I work until I drop. He wanted me to not place unfeeling, unseeing, powerless idols in His place.

I normally ace tests. But on this test, the most important test of my life to date, the test that asked if would I continue to affirm that God was enough, no matter how dire the circumstance, I had failed miserably.

As I continued to confront the enormity of my betrayal of God, I came across the story of another Christian who went through terrible suffering.

His name was Horatio Spafford, and he wrote the great old hymn "It Is Well With My Soul." He and his wife Anna were well known in the Chicago area in the 1860's. He was a lawyer and a businessman. But money did not insulate him from tragedy. In 1870 their only son was killed by scarlet fever at the age of four. A year later the Great Chicago Fire struck, and most of Horatio's real estate holdings were destroyed. He decided that a holiday to England would be good for the whole family. He and Anna had four daughters, and in 1873 he put them on the ship the "Ville de Havre" to Europe. At the last minute a business challenge prevented him from sailing with them, but he insisted they go ahead, he would join them later. On November 2, 1873, the "Ville de Havre" collided with another ship in the middle of the Atlantic, and sank in only 12 minutes, claiming the lives of 226 people, including all four of the Spafford daughters. Anna was saved only because a plank floated underneath her and propped up her unconscious body.

When Horatio heard the dreadful news, he

boarded the next ship out of New York. We are told that during the voyage the captain called Mr. Spafford to the bridge. He told him that by best reckoning they were at the place where the de Havre sank, and where his daughters lay in their watery grave. Horatio returned to his cabin, and wrote this hymn.

When peace, like a river, attendeth my way,
when sorrows, like sea billows roll;
whatever my lot, Thou has taught me to
say, it is well, it is well, with my soul.

Though Satan should buffet, though trials
should come, let this blessed assurance
control, that Christ has regarded my
helpless estate,
and hath shed His own blood for my soul.

My sin, oh, the bliss of this glorious
thought! My sin, not in part, but in whole,
is nailed to the cross, and I bear it no more,
praise the Lord, praise the Lord, O my soul!

And Lord, haste the day when my faith shall

be sight, the clouds be rolled back as a scroll; The trumpet shall sound, and the Lord shall descend, even so, it is well with my soul.

In the midst of his almost unthinkable personal loss, Horatio Spafford affirmed that God was enough.

Isn't is almost shocking to consider that a human being, having had the experience of Spafford, could write what he did in this hymn? How could it be "well with his soul" in the midst of such an experience!? It could be well with his soul because the health and welfare of his children had not become an idol in his heart.

What if that had been my sons, or my grandbabies? I would have relived their experience in my imagination at least 1000 times a day. I would have died with them over and over again. I would have felt the icy ocean water that must have struck their bodies like a brick wall. I would have panicked with them as the salt water stung their eyes, filled their ears, and inexorably smothered their lungs. I would have drowned with them 1000 times as the fight finally left their bodies, and they sank, down down down into the inky darkness.

Spafford's story reminded me of a nightmare I had when Jedd was a toddler. In my dream Jedd had somehow escaped my grasp, and I could not find him. I ran along paths, through some kind of a park, calling for him, screaming for him, but I could not find him. After what seemed like an eternity, I saw ahead of me, off to the side, something under a bush, something that looked like my little son, lying there. I crept closer, my heart pounding with terror. But before I could get there, I woke up. My poor husband. I woke him in hysterics, sobbing and shaking. We had to go into Jedd's nursery to assure me that he was there, that he was ok, that he had not been molested, or injured, or murdered. There he was in his crib, curled tightly into a ball, his blond hair curling damply on his head, his chubby little cheek flushed with sleep. Back in bed, Mike held me for hours before I calmed down enough to go back to sleep. But what if that had not been just a bad dream, but a terrible reality. Would my response have been "it is well with my soul"?

Clearly not! I had proved through these couple of decades of loss that that would NOT have been my response. I was continuing to see the awful gravity of my unfaithfulness. I was continuing to see the idols I had embraced. I had lost things only, nothing so precious as a child or grandchild. But I had accused God of being uncaring and unfeeling, instead of embracing his "enough-ness" in the midst of the trials and struggles of life.

I am certain Horatio Spafford's affirmation came through wrenching tears and unspeakable pain. He wasn't being Pollyanna when he wrote this hymn. He wasn't in denial either. Rather, he was reaching down into his soul to the one unshakeable Reality that was bigger and stronger than his grief and sorrow, and finding there the only comfort adequate to such a moment.

Rather than accusing God as I had done, he was able to embrace God's faithfulness in the midst of the tragedy and unfairness of life. He knew that God's goodness wasn't dependent on things going well in his life. He believed that the same kind, compassionate Jesus of the Bible who wept with those who wept, was also weeping with him - so it was well with his soul. He wasn't alone in his pain but had a Friend holding his hand Who had suffered more than he did or ever would.

I had gone days, months, years where it was so easy to know that God was enough. He seemed so present, so right at hand, so accessible. Then in a day, in a moment, the sky turned dark. The sun disappeared. The rain fell in impenetrable torrents. I got hit by a baseball bat, right across the head, not just once, but bash, bash, bash, time after time. God was right there, but I was blind to his presence. I could no longer reach out and feel Him. But He had not left me, I had left Him. His faithfulness had not altered, mine had. I had replaced Him with unworthy and uncaring idols.

I was beginning to see not just the foolishness and the stupidity, but the horror of what I had done. I had exchanged the living, loving, eternally faithful, magnificent, attentive Creator, the Lover of my soul, the one who had held on to me through thick and thin, for lifeless, dumb idols. Idols that in the great scheme of things are temporary and insignificant. Let me reiterate that these things are not wrong in themselves. Jesus assures us that God knows our wants and needs, and affirms their importance. But it is a matter of what comes first in my life. Do I look to God to make my life complete and meaningful? Or do I look to something else, anything else; money, security, even the welfare of my children?

This is not hypothetical rhetoric to me. Tyler is a single Dad with sole responsibility for his two little ones, and like me, he works on commission. Jedd has been unemployed for over two years now, and Teri makes most of their income on commission. This economy has not been kind to commission based sales people! So I go to bed every night knowing that there is a good chance that my grandchildren went to bed hungry. Or that their parents didn't eat so they could. Can you feel how this breaks my heart? Mike and I face the very real possibility of not being able to afford the apartment we are living in. But as with Job, God is showing me again that the one thing, the only thing that really matters, is my relationship with Him. He is still enough, if only I would crawl back into His arms. And He had not given up on me. He was inexorably and wonderfully pulling me back to Himself. He loves me, He knows what will satisfy me. He knows that only He is enough, and He was no longer going to let me forget it. As I write this, I am still in the midst of this process. I am still facing and repenting of the way I accused God, of how I turned my back on Him when the going got too tough.

But Psalm 73 does not end in the acknowledgement of unbelief and failure. The writer goes on, just as if he was in this present day journey with me.

"Yet I am always with you; you hold me by my right hand. You guide me with your counsel, and afterward you will take me into glory. Whom have I in heaven but you? And being with you, I desire nothing on earth. My flesh and my heart may fail, but God is the strength of my heart and my portion forever."

Another translation of this verse says "When my skin sags and my bones get brittle, God is rock solid and faithful."

From across the centuries, the writer of this Psalm had questioned God when his losses became more than he could handle. Just like me, he had turned from God, and had become brutish and dumb. But just like me, God had pulled him back to the only reality that makes going on with life meaningful and possible. "Whom have I in heaven but you? And being with you, I desire nothing on earth." In plain English, there is no one in heaven or on earth who satisfies like Jesus. God was drawing me back to him, expelling my idols for me, and I was once again feeling and reveling in the truth that not only is God enough, He is all there is.

19 BUT IF NOT

The other day Mike and I took the two hour drive into California's central valley to go shopping for RV's. No, not shopping, we are not there yet. Looking. Trying to visualize what it might be like to live in one. We are still a few weeks away from having to make such a decision, but we know that my current income is not enough to allow us to sign a new lease on this apartment. So our thinking is that instead of using the last of my little 401K to pay rent, it would make more sense to use it to buy an old RV. At least we would have something to show for our money, and we could live in it instead of in our car. Plus it was raining in Santa Rosa, and there was sunshine in the central valley,

Our kids are in a state of unbelief about the whole process. Like me, they have a vivid mental picture of Mike and I chugging down the highway, in an old RV, singing "Hit the road, Jack! Bada bump, bada bump, bada bump, bada bump, hit the road, Jack!" Tyler said we should come live with him and his kids in his apartment. Yeah, that really sounds like fun. Jedd said "Is it really that bad?" And our daughter-in-law Teri sighed and said "How the mighty have fallen." Anyway, for a vehicle that is so monstrously huge on the outside, RVs are very small on the inside. I had actually never been inside one before. It was quite a revelation. The best way to visualize the shower is to think of the diameter of your average trash can. Add some height, and you get a pretty accurate picture. Plus Mikey was explaining to me that you do not leave the water running while you take a shower. He said that you leave the water on only long enough to get wet, then turn it off, soap up, and turn it back on when you are ready to rinse off. Oh boy. A long hot luxurious shower is something I give sincere thanks for every morning. Then there's the kitchen. There is a very small stove, an even smaller sink, and about six inches of counter space. How would Mike possibly manage one of his wonderful meals is such a truncated space! I was starting to hyper-ventilate. Most of the older RVs we looked at had no closet at all, let alone any place to hang my suits or our coats. Mikey kept reminding me that with all their limitations, an RV is substantially more spacious than our Scion!

We had not been on the road back home long before Mike started down the "if only" path. He knows better, but he couldn't help himself. Sticking my fingers in my ears and yelling "neener neener neener" did not stop him. The list was long. If only we had stayed in that first little house we bought in Seattle in 1976. If only we had stayed in the first house we built in Kirkland. If only we had never left the pink house. If only we had never started the furniture company. If only we had never sold the condo, or at least had bought our little rambler, but been content to live in it as it was instead of doing the remodel. How about if only we had never had kids! Think of all the money that would have saved us over the years!

Mike needed to vent about this for a while, but then we started to grin at each other, and finally laugh. We both know that we are smack in the middle of God's plan for our life, that God is intimately involved, that He is walking with us as we contemplate this unfamiliar and daunting new direction.

So we are not going to indulge in the "if only" thing. But we are going to affirm a little gem of truth we recently re-discovered in the Old Testament. This gem of truth is contained in the phrase "But if not."

The statement "but if not" comes from one of my favorite events recorded in the Bible. It is the report about three Jewish men who lived and served under Nebuchadnezzar, one of the mighty kings of Babylon, which was one of the great civilizations of the ancient world. The king decided to have a huge statue of himself made of gold, and then invited all the government's officials and bureaucrats from his entire kingdom to the dedication of the statue. I use the word invited advisedly. If you cared about not being torn limb from limb you would absolutely attend. In Nebuchadnezzar's day you did not simply send your excuses.

It was made clear that when everyone gathered for the dedication, and the orchestra played, everyone was to bow down and worship this statue. If anyone were to refuse, he would be thrown without delay into the midst of a burning fiery furnace. Nothing like a taste of good old fashioned middle eastern despotism. So it is no surprise that when the orchestra struck up the ancient equivalent of "Hail to the Chief", everyone hit the ground. Everyone that is, except, our three Jewish heroes. Their names were Shadrach, Meshach, and Abednego. My boys used to call them Your Shack, My Shack, and To Bed We Go. These men were important officials in the King's service, so other jealous officials were eager to report their disobedience to the King. Nebuchadnezzar was furious, but He was willing to give them one more chance. He told Shadrach, Meshach, and Abednego that he would have the music played one more time, but if they did not bow down and worship his golden image this time, the furnace would be their fate. He concluded his threat by saying, "Then what god will be able to rescue you from my hand?"

Imagine yourself in that place. I would think of all the good I could do if I stayed alive. Not to mention, I am standing in front of the most powerful man on earth at that time. These guys were facing not just deprivation and difficulty, they were facing certain death. This was not will I, or will I not, live my last days in an RV, this was will I live at all. In that kind of dire situation, the threat often seems much more real than an invisible God. But not to Shadrach, Meshach, and Abednego. These men proved that they knew the God they worshipped. It wasn't just religion for them. They had a relationship with the God of the Bible, and they owed Him their complete loyalty, irrespective of the consequences. We don't know how they felt at that moment. They might have been brave, or they might have been shaking in their boots. But this is what they said. "If we are thrown into the blazing furnace, the God we serve is able to save us from it, and He will rescue us from your hand, O King. *But if not* we want you to know, O King, that we will not serve your gods or worship the image of gold you have set up." "But if not." Three tiny little words, eight letters, that put the entire world into perspective. These words reveal the heart of men who understood with clarity and conviction that God is, that God is good, that He is faithful and trustworthy, that He is powerful and able to deliver. Yet they also understood that you don't always know how God will act in any given moment. You don't always know if he will extricate you from a particular sticky wicket. Regardless of the outcome, God Himself, God alone, was enough for them. And they would not betray Him, even if it cost them their lives.

Their response so infuriated Nebuchadnezzar that he had the furnace heated seven times hotter than usual. It was so hot in fact, that the men given the dubious honor of throwing the shackled Shadrach, Meshach, and Abednego into the fire were themselves incinerated. But as the King looked into the fire he saw that there were not three, but four men there, walking around, unbound and unharmed. He was amazed! He said, "...the fourth looks like a son of the gods." He called to our men to "...come out of there." When they emerged, the King's advisors crowded around them, and saw that the fire had not harmed their bodies, or singed their hair; their robes were not scorched, and there was no smell of fire on them. The King had a serious pivotal moment. "Praise be to the God of Shadrach, Meshach, and Abednego," he said "who has sent his angel and rescued his servants! They trusted in Him and defied the king's command, and were willing to give up their lives rather than serve or worship any god except their own God."

Life throws stuff at us. Usually the consequences are not as dire and immediate as a fiery furnace, but sometimes they are. I do not want to minimize the struggle. Your son is killed in a car wreck. You lose your job, your money, all your assets. You get cancer. These things seem beyond our ability to endure. It often feels like we are in the furnace and getting burned. And we don't see the fourth person, who is right there in the furnace with us.

For Shadrach, Meshach, and Abednego,

whether they got burned or not wasn't the point. We all hope, like them, for a happy outcome. BUT IF NOT, even if God does not intervene, He is still enough.

20 GOD IS ENOUGH

Your first clue that I have been in the furniture industry too long is that I visualize the true truth that "God is enough" as a table. But not just any table; a large, round, sturdy, bespoke, family table. It is built of solid planks of real wood, thick and robust, joined together to form a table that welcomes the banging of grandbabies' spoons, the pounding of argumentative fists, the clinking of glasses, the scraping of chairs in and out, and the ongoing succession of platter after platter groaning with sustenance.

This is not a table that is suspended firmly in thin air. This is not a leap of faith table. This is a table that sits immoveable and indestructible on four solid, beautifully carved, substantial legs. This is a magnanimous table. It never runs out of room. There is always room at this table for a hungry heart, an under nourished soul, a battered seeker. The four legs that support this table have names. And because it is a round table, each leg holds equal responsibility, equal weight.

The first leg is named "God Is". This is the leg that affirms what I learned from Francis Schaeffer, that the God of the Bible is the only reasonable and thoughtful explanation for man's existence, personality, and moral dilemma. God is enough quite simply because HE IS, and without Him life has no meaning, no relief from absurdity, no significance.

The second leg is named "God Is Worthy." Job reminds me of this. In his moment of deep despair God showed Himself to Job. Do you remember how Job responded? He replied to God, "My ears had heard of you, but now my eyes have seen you. Therefore I despise myself and repent in sack cloth and ashes." He went on to say "Though God slay me, yet will I hope in Him." Job reminds me that my God is a mighty God, a good God, a transcendent God, a faithful God, the God who created me; the God who alone is enough to satisfy the deepest longings of my heart.

The third leg on the table "God is enough" is named "God Loves Me." Ok, what can there be that is better than that! What could be more enough than being loved by the God who created you! God has so faithfully, so long, and so enduringly loved me. He has demonstrated His love for me in all the ways you have seen in my story. You probably realize that I have the best husband on the face of the planet. He has cherished me for almost forty years now, and his love has been a homing beacon in my life. But his love is not enough. It is not enough to meet the basic needs of my life, to satisfy the deepest longings of my heart. God's love is, however, quite enough to do exactly that.

The fourth leg is named "God Gives Me Hope and a Future." This life is not all there is. Horatio Spafford got this. Remember the last verse of that hymn he wrote while over his daughters' grave?

"O Lord, haste the day when my faith shall be sight;

The clouds be rolled back as a scroll.

The trumpet shall sound and

the Lord shall descend!

Even so, it is well with my soul."

The end of my life is not going to be when I slowly rot into the landscape along with my RV. This life is only a shadow, a premonition, of the life that awaits; a life where I will walk with Jesus, will see Him face to face, and will understand in a way I cannot even begin to grasp now, what it means that He is enough.

Four legs. Four faithful, true truth legs, that buttress the God is enough table. God Is, God Is Worthy, God Loves Me, and God Gives Me Hope and a Future. This is why God is enough. This is why He satisfies like nothing else.

But here's the rub. This table, this God is enough table, is one that I can choose to push my chair away from. And I did just that for a period of time. A miserable, angry, debilitating period of time. But I am back at that table. The chair with my name on it was waiting for me, willing me to come back and sit down. I have glued myself to that seat. I am sitting at that table, upright and expectant, fork in one hand and knife in the other, ready for whatever fare God serves me next.

This is not a story about me finally getting it right. It's a story about the faithfulness of God. There is no guarantee that I won't get it wrong again. You can tell that I am still in the midst of my life story, with many things unresolved, and many chances still ahead for me to react in faith or non faith. As I get to know myself better, year after year, and get to know God better, year after year, I come to understand how, in large and small ways, I get it wrong daily. But I also see an immensely faithful God, whose invitation to his table is always open. Jesus is the fourth man in the furnace, always there whether or not I see Him or feel Him. He is faithful to His promise to be with me, to forgive me, to restore me. He is faithful to hold my hand even when I let go of His. He is faithful to wait, month after month, year after year, for me to come back to his table.

Mike and I still face uncomfortable issues. We do not want to end up living in an RV, or a trailer park, or - God forbid - in our Scion. But if we do end up in our Scion, I can tell you this; God has done in these last few months a restorative and transforming work in my heart that will allow me to scramble up on the hood of my car, throw my arms wide, and proclaim at the top of my voice to any who will give ear, "This is OK, because God is enough!" "God loves me and that is enough!" "God is with me in my Scion, and that is enough!"

"Whom have I in heaven but you? And being with you, I desire nothing on earth. My flesh and my heart may fail, but God is the strength of my heart and my portion forever."

AFTERWORD

Dear reader, if you have gotten this far into my book, you have taken quite a journey with me. Thank you for that. Now let's talk. All of you have had your own journeys, some much more difficult than mine, some easier. The point of this book is not that religion is the way to survive these journeys. This is *not* about religion. Religion is man's attempt to gain God's favor. Religion attempts to do something, anything to fill the great void we all feel when we live apart from our Creator. Religion is when we enter into frenetic activity in an attempt to smother the emptiness and horror of our existence. Religion is our attempt to be enough, to find enough in ourselves to make sense of life, to survive life. Religion is never enough to meet our basic screaming need for God.

God being enough is about relationship. Relationship with the God who IS THERE, the God who stands waiting to offer you comfort, purpose, meaning, shelter, help, encouragement, rescue, completeness. This is not a religious God. This is not a God who demands cowering, or groveling, or self loathing. This is not a God who relishes punishment, or who cracks the stone tablet of law over your head. This is a God who Himself, in Jesus Christ, paid the penalty for our sin, our anger, our rebellion - like those very painful things I shared with you about myself. The Bible says about Jesus that "He took up our infirmities and carried our sorrows. He was pierced for our transgressions, he was crushed for our iniquities; the punishment that brought us peace was upon him, and by his wounds we are healed. We all like sheep have gone astray, each of us has turned to his own way; and the Lord laid on Him the iniquity of us all."

This is a God who invites you, because of what Jesus did, to be in relationship with Him. This is a God who bends to you, who wants to look you in the eye and envelop you in His forgiveness and love. He is eager to give you hope and a future. You can respond to His invitation simply by reaching out to Him in faith. That means you place your trust in Him. You clutch his hand.

You tell Him you can no longer go it alone. And you let Him wash your sin and guilt away. Then you will find out bit by bit, and step by step, that only He is enough for all that life has brought and will bring your way. If Mike and I can help you in this process please feel free to contact us at *isGodenough@gmail.com*

Acknowledgments:

I owe my husband Mike huge thanks for his help in clarifying and amplifying the more theological portions of this book; my friend Jason DesLongchamp for his critical contributions; and Gib Martin and Larry Richards for their invaluable encouragement, counsel, and insight in making this a more mature work.

I have to also thank Mike for telling me this book wasn't done, even when I was sure it was; for allowing such transparency about his life; and for giving so much of his time and energy to help me bring this book to completion.

About the author:

Becky graduated cum laude from Westmont College, in Santa Barbara, California, where she met her husband of 39 years. Her calling has been to serve God as a wife, mother, and grandmother, and as a pastor's wife and interior designer. As a pastor's wife she helped her husband live out their vision for an honest faith, manifested in authentic Christian community. As an interior designer and sales person her purpose has been to bring God's love of creativity and hospitality to everyday home life. She has consistently been at the top of her profession, with many interiors published in national shelter magazines. She has been frequently sought out for interviews and for sales training videos in her field. This is her first book, but not her last.

8932961R0

Made in the USA
Charleston, SC
27 July 2011